PRAISE FOR THE WO

MW00488797

In this beautiful book, Rabbi Rami invites us to step outside of ourselves to taste the truth as understood by the great religious traditions.

—Rabbi Ellen Bernstein, author of *Splendor of Creation*, and founder of Shomrei Adamah, Keepers of the Earth

This book is a treasure. Whatever your spiritual path, *The World Wisdom Bible* will give you a deeper knowing of the Truth that weaves through all existence.

—Rabbi Stephen Booth-Nadav, Director, Wisdom House Denver: A Center for Multifaith Engagement and Spiritual Inquiry

The World Wisdom Bible is a testament of the internal pilgrimage of souls down the ages and around the globe. Here, we too can find our soul's yearnings mirrored, encouraged, and consoled. It is an invaluable reference for travelers, a companion for those on the way.

—Sister Jo-Ann Iannotti, OP, Art and Spirituality Director, Wisdom House Retreat and Conference Center

The World Wisdom Bible is a treasure whose time has come.

—Rev. Barbara Brown Taylor, author of *Leaving Church* and *Holy Envy* (forthcoming)

The World Wisdom Bible touches the soul and mind of the spiritual seeker who yearns to move beyond doctrine into the grandeur of divine space.

—Sister Rosemarie Greco, DW, Executive Director Wisdom House Retreat and Conference Center

The World Wisdom Bible is a multicolored tapestry woven from the vibrant threads of the world's spiritual traditions helping us to find universal meaning to guide our lives.

—Ed Bastian, author of *Living Fully Dying Well* and *InterSpiritual Meditation*

THE

WORLD
WISDOM

BIBLE

A New Testament for
a Global Spirituality

Presented by the
One River Foundation

Edited by Rami Shapiro
Editor and Annotator,
Perennial Wisdom for the Spiritually Independent

Foreword by Mirabai Starr
Author, *God of Love:*
A Guide to the Heart of Judaism, Christianity and Islam

Walking Together, Finding the Way®

SKYLIGHT PATHS®
PUBLISHING
Nashville, Tennessee

SkyLight Paths Publishing
an imprint of Turner Publishing Company
Nashville, Tennessee
New York, New York

www.skylightpaths.com
www.turnerpublishing.com

The World Wisdom Bible:
A New Testament for a Global Spirituality

2017 Quality Paperback Edition, First Printing
© 2017 by One River Foundation

For information regarding permission to reprint material from this book, please write or fax your request to Turner Publishing, Permissions Department, at 4507 Charlotte Avenue, Nashville, Tennessee, (615) 255-2665, fax (615) 255-5081, or email your request to submissions@turnerpublishing.com.

Library of Congress Cataloging-in-Publication Data
Names: Shapiro, Rami M., editor.
Title: The world wisdom bible : a new testament for a global spirituality /
   presented by the One River Foundation ; edited by Rami Shapiro ; editor
   and annotator, Perennial Wisdom for the Spiritually Independent.
Description: Quality Paperback Edition. | Nashville : Turner Publishing
   Company, 2017. | Includes bibliographical references.
Identifiers: LCCN 2016052461 | ISBN 9781594736360 (pbk. : alk. paper)
Subjects: LCSH: Sacred books.
Classification: LCC BL70 .W67 2017 | DDC 208/.2--dc23
LC record available at https://lccn.loc.gov/2016052461

10 9 8 7 6 5 4 3 2 1

Manufactured in the United States of America
Cover Design: Thor Goodrich
Interior Design: Tim Holtz

"If we are to have peace on earth, our loyalties must become ecumenical rather than sectional. Our loyalties must transcend our race, our tribe, our class, and our nation; and this means we must develop a world perspective."

—Martin Luther King Jr., sermon at Ebenezer Baptist Church, Atlanta, Georgia, December 25, 1967

"Twenty-five hundred years ago it took an exceptional individual like Diogenes to exclaim, '*I am not an Athenian or a Greek but a citizen of the world*.' Today we must all be struggling to make those words our own."

—Huston Smith, *The Illustrated World's Religions: A Guide to Our Wisdom Traditions*

To all those whose loyalty to Truth
takes them beyond the boundaries of sacred opinion.

Contents

Foreword, by Mirabai Starr vii

Preface: What Is *The World Wisdom Bible*? ix

Acknowledgments xi

The World Wisdom Bible Advisory Counsel xiii

A Note on Translation xv

A Note on God xvii

Introduction xix

Chapter One — Ultimate Reality
Recognizing the One That Is All 1

Chapter Two — The Eternal I
Understanding God-Consciousness 17

Chapter Three — The Self or Mind
Awakening to Your Divine Nature 29

Chapter Four — The Nature of Wisdom
Overcoming the Illusion of Separateness 35

Chapter Five — Who Are the Wise?
Identifying the Voices of Wisdom 43

Chapter Six — The Way
Discovering a Path to Wisdom 59

Chapter Seven — Living Wisely
Dwelling in Wisdom from Day to Day 95

Chapter Eight — Dying Wisely
Returning to the One 129

Appendix One   Warnings from the Dark Side:
                Scriptures of Hate, Fear, and Violence   139

Appendix Two   The Eight Points of Agreement   150

Appendix Three Universal Declaration of Human Rights   153

        Notes   161

        Sages Cited, Annotated   162

        Primary Sources, Annotated   173

        Bibliography and Suggestions for Further Reading   187

Foreword

Mirabai Starr

This book is more than a collection of wise words; it is the song of the human heart. It is the cry of the despairing for solace and of the outraged for justice, and it is a gasp of holy awe. These words lead us beyond language to the place from which all wisdom arises and to the wholeness that is our birthright.

And who are we, the guests at this great feast? We come from everywhere, and we find the One wherever we are: inside the sacred spaces of each of the world's faiths and out in the wild places of the earth; shoulder to shoulder in the mosque, bending to press our hearts to the ground in surrender; in the haunting melodies of our ancestors as we call on the Shekinah to infuse us with her indwelling feminine spirit on Shabbat; in the Communion bread and wine, which we take in remembrance of the Prince of Peace. We hear the voice of the One joining with ours when we chant the divine names in Sanskrit and Tibetan, Hebrew and Latin and Arabic. We feel the breath of the One against our face in the luminous silence of Zen meditation halls and coursing through our bodies when we pray for healing. We notice that there is nowhere the One is not—even in utter formlessness, where we recognize that we are not separate from that which we long for and that we are fundamentally interdependent with all that is.

Rabbi Rami Shapiro and his team have taken great care to comb the scriptures of the world's religions for the most potent and relevant teachings for our times. Taoism offers context for the entire spiritual enterprise in the opening lines of the Tao Te Ching: *The Tao that can be told is not the eternal Tao.* Buddhism affirms that there is only one of us, and therefore we are each responsible for every link in the web of being. Christianity offers us the unconditional mercy of an incarnational God who permeates the whole of creation with love. Judaism urges us to demonstrate our love for God in the way we treat each other and care for creation. Hinduism kindles the fire of devotion for reunification with the Beloved who is no other than our own true Self. Islam shares the peace that comes with complete submission to the One.

I had the good fortune to come of age in a time and place where I was exposed to the heart of diverse wisdom traditions—Hinduism, Buddhism, Sufism, mystical Judaism, Christian mysticism, Native American spirituality—and encouraged to say yes to them all. I was also taught to wrestle, like our ancestor Jacob-who-became-Israel, with every angel I encountered. This continual dance of inquiry honed my faculty of discrimination and protected me against the temptation to build a cage of beliefs and go to sleep there. I learned that to open my heart to the presence of the sacred wherever I caught a whiff of its fragrance meant cultivating ferocious courage. Saying yes to love meant saying no to hatred, to racism and sexism, to the oppression of the marginalized and the comfort of the privileged. It also rendered me incapable of picking one religion to the exclusion of the others. Becoming a "something" felt like a violation of my pact to follow the Beloved wherever the Beloved led me.

And the Beloved has taken me to the holy houses of every one of the world's major religions and to a few of its more hidden ones. As a professor of religious studies and a translator of the mystics, I have spent countless hours reading the sacred texts of all faiths and the ecstatic poetry that came through its mystics. I have glimpsed the same shining thread running throughout the tapestry of our perennial wisdom legacy and appreciated the diverse ways in which we sing the one song of the human heart. It has become clear to me that while the world's religions cannot and must not be reduced to one truth, their core teachings are unifying; they are all calling us to the truth of our essential oneness. This unity in diversity is a cause for celebration.

The World Wisdom Bible is an invitation to that celebration. It is a joyful noise, a fertile silence, a prophetic call, a beautiful fever, a blessed remedy, and the promise of hope for our troubled times. No single tradition will draw us a map to guide us through the wilderness of the human condition. But together, all the world's wisdom ways illuminate a path to lead us home.

Preface

What Is *The World Wisdom Bible*?

Humanity stands at a spiritual crossroads. Turn one way, and we fall deeper into ignorance, fear, alienation, and chaos. Turn another way, and we lift ourselves up toward wisdom, love, unity, and peace. There are powerful forces pushing us in each direction, and there is no guarantee as to which way we will choose. Yet as Rabbi Tarfon taught two thousand years ago, while "[we] are not obligated to complete the task [of perfecting humanity], nor are [we] free to abandon it" (*Pirke Avot* 2:21). *The World Wisdom Bible* is part of the process of perfection.

In approaching this project, we at the One River Foundation take our inspiration from the dedicated folks at Gideon International who have been placing Christian Bibles in hospital and hotel rooms around the world for over one hundred years. Like the Gideons, we believe ideas matter. We believe that having access to a physical book of spiritual insight can change lives. We understand that hospitals and hotels are often places of deep alienation and loneliness where we confront life's most challenging questions: *Who am I? Where did I come from? Where am I going when I die? How should I live while alive, and why?* We understand that a wise word at such moments can open hearts, change minds, and ignite the courage to move through the crises of our lives.

Where we differ from the Gideons is in limiting that wise word to the Protestant Bible. Where the Gideons seek to place the New Testament of the Christian faith in every guest room, we seek to place a new testament of global spirituality right next to it. Where they hope to expand the reach of one religion, we seek to spread the perennial wisdom shared by the great saints, sages, and mystics of all religions. We are not seeking to replace the Gideon Bible but to share the drawer in which it rests.

While *The World Wisdom Bible* is sold in bookstores and online, our greater goal is to offer free copies of this book to hospitals, hotels, guest houses, religious institutions, retreat centers, and other places of spiritual seeking. We invite you to help us achieve this goal by becoming a Friend of *The World Wisdom Bible* (www.worldwisdombible.org) and joining our network of donors and distributors who help us purchase copies in bulk and offer them at no cost to public and private institutions in their own communities.

Acknowledgments

*T*he *World Wisdom Bible* grew out of a blog post by Rabbi Rami Shapiro in which he imagined an interspiritual alternative to the Gideon Bible one finds in hotel rooms around the globe. Among those who read the post, Frank Levy responded and asked how he could help. At the time there was nothing to help with; on the contrary, what was needed was for someone to take the idea to fruition. It is this task that Frank took on. As *The World Wisdom Bible* took on its final form we sought out our friend and teacher Mirabai Starr to write the Foreword. We wanted a voice as deep and wise as any found in the Bible to be the opening voice of the Bible. Mirabai thank you so much for your words and support.

Having someone at the helm of *The World Wisdom Bible* project meant that we had good chance of pulling this off. But it also meant we needed a "this," an actual *World Wisdom Bible* that could be read and placed in hotel rooms next to its older cousin, the Gideon. Enter Emily Wichland and SkyLight Paths, a division of Turner Publishing.

Emily has edited over a dozen of Rabbi Rami's books, and while the Gideon model of sales and distribution was something neither she nor the good folks at SkyLight Paths had ever tackled before, they embraced it. Moreover, they provided us with the translations of the texts we needed from their award-winning SkyLight Illuminations series of classic religious texts. While our hope is to translate *The World Wisdom Bible* into dozens of languages over time, having access to these fine English translations was a huge boost to the project.

As the writing and compilation progressed toward completion, we turned to Aaron Shapiro, a professor of English at Middle Tennessee State University, to help with the editing and to write its annotated "Sages Cited, Annotated" and "Primary Sources, Annotated" sections, a task he had done so effectively in *Perennial Wisdom for the Spiritually Independent: Sacred Teachings—Annotated and Explained* (SkyLight Paths), the forerunner and companion to *The World Wisdom Bible*. We also reached out to Kabir and Camille Helminski, founders and directors of the Threshold Society, who gave us permission to draw from Camille's *The Light of Dawn: Daily Readings from the Holy Qur'an*, her excellent translation of Qur'anic verse.

The World Wisdom Bible is part of a larger effort to share the perennial wisdom of the world's religions that includes online forums, portals to the great books of human spirituality, and retreats with Rabbi Rami. To create and maintain a dynamic web presence, we turned to Rev. Claire Goodman, who understands not only the sacred teachings but also how to market and distribute them in the digital world.

We are most grateful to Frank, Emily, Aaron, Kabir, Camille, and Claire for their help.

Last but certainly not least, we are grateful to our ever-growing network of Friends of *The World Wisdom Bible*, who supplied the start-up capital for—and who continue to fund—this project and to seed copies of *The World Wisdom Bible* in their communities.

Thanks to everyone who has made *The World Wisdom Bible* a reality and to those of you who are new to the project, who find yourselves called to participate as well.

The World Wisdom Bible
Advisory Council

The role of our advisory council is threefold:

1. To suggest texts and teachings from their respective religious traditions that we can add to *The World Wisdom Bible* website
2. To promote the importance of *The World Wisdom Bible* to their constituencies
3. To help brainstorm the future of *The World Wisdom Bible* project and its ongoing effort to enhance spiritual literacy and shift religious wisdom from the parochial to the perennial

We are grateful to the following scholars and clergy for their continuing efforts:

Swami Atmarupananda
Sheikh Ossama Bahloul
Dr. Ed Bastian
Rabbi Alexis Berk
Rabbi Ellen Bernstein
Rabbi Stephen Booth-Nadav
Rev. Cynthia Bourgeault
Sr. Pravrajika Brahmaprana
Fr. Matthew Fox
Rev. Claire Goodman
Sr. Rosemarie Greco, DW
Sheikha Camille Helminski
Sheikh Kabir Helminski
Sr. Jo-Ann Iannotti, OP

Thomas Moore
Yogacharya O'Brian
Fr. Gordon Peerman
Rev. Dan Rosemergy
Fr. John Runkle
Mirabai Starr
Swami Yogatmananda

A Note on Translation

The texts of *The World Wisdom Bible* are drawn from many different sources and bear the mark of many different translators. All of the texts compiled here reference the source from which they were taken as well as the names of the translators. Special thanks are due to the many translators of the SkyLight Illuminations series: Yusuf Ali, Stevan Davies, Ibrahim Gamard, Livia Kohn, Donald Kraus, Sheryl Kujawa-Holbrook, James Legge, Derek Lin, Ron Miller, Max Müller, Andrew Philip Smith, and Shri Purohit Swami. Those texts not referencing a specific translator were translated by Rabbi Rami Shapiro.

While all the texts of *The World Wisdom Bible* speak to aspects of perennial wisdom, no attempt was made to blend these texts into a unified voice—with a handful of exceptions. First, we took the liberty of editing the material for gender neutrality and inclusivity whenever this could be done without confusing the sense of the original text. These texts are ancient and cannot be expected to reflect the social realities of our own time. *The World Wisdom Bible*, however, is a contemporary spiritual testament that does speak to our time, and because it does, we made changes that aim to eliminate the inherent male bias reflected in most of these texts. We did this by rendering plural what was originally singular (changing "he" to "they") and putting in the second person what was originally in the third person (changing "he" and "his" to "you" and "your"), as well as by changing gender-specific nouns, such as "Father," to non-gendered nouns, such as the "One," thus allowing us to broaden the audience of these texts without altering their meaning or message.

Second, we took some liberty with presentation—all translations are presented in verse format—as well as with punctuation. We are aware of the conventional ways of marking deletions from texts; however, readability was our key concern. Too many grammatical marks would be distracting for the reader, and as this is not intended to be an academic work, we chose to omit them.

Finally, some of the diction in the translations has also been altered. Here, the clarity of the texts was our primary concern, and changes were made to better facilitate the comprehension of contemporary readers. In all cases, however, great care was taken to maintain fidelity to the spirit of the original passages. We have, of course, provided a citation with each excerpt so that readers interested in the original wording can easily find the source texts.

A Note on God

The World Wisdom Bible speaks of God in three ways: Ultimate Reality, the Eternal I, and the Self. Each is a different finger pointing toward what the sixth-century-BCE Chinese philosopher and poet Lao Tzu called the *Tao that cannot be named*. This is the Truth beyond any -ism or ideology, dogma or creed, religion or system of belief. This is what Chan Buddhism calls "suchness," or *tathātā*.

Suchness is not mysterious, though it is often wondrous. It is what is; what the Hebrew Bible calls YHVH—a phrase usually translated as "I am who I am," but perhaps better translated as "I will be what I will be"—and as such indicative of the happening of all happening, the source and substance of being itself as it unfolds in time (Exodus 3:14). Both awesome and terrifying, it is the ground of all existence, the fountain of light and dark, good and evil, everything and its opposite (Job 2:10; Isaiah 45:7; Bhagavad Gita 11:7,13). It is what the Pharisees of Jesus's time called the Place, *HaMakom*, of all being and becoming and what the apostle Paul referred to as that in which "we live and move and have our being" (Acts 17:28). It is the seen and the unseen; the known, the unknown, and the unknowable. It is the preciousness of this and every moment when we realize that life is, as Buddha taught, "but a breath,"[1] and reality is, as the Hebrew sage Ecclesiastes (*Koheleth*) wrote, as impermanent as the morning dew (Ecclesiastes 6:12).

When we speak of *tathātā* as Ultimate Reality, we speak of the infinite whole that includes and transcends all finite reality. When we speak of *tathātā* as the Self, we speak of the part that knows itself to be an expression of this infinite whole, and therefore one with the whole. When we give voice to or listen to (but never talk about, precisely because, due to its nature, it cannot be spoken about) *tathātā* as the Eternal I, we shift from

God as absolute object (Ultimate Reality and Self) to God as pure Subject that cannot be made into an object of any kind.

One way to understand this is to imagine Ultimate Reality as an infinite ocean, the Self as a wave of that ocean that knows itself to be one with all other waves and the infinite ocean itself, and the Eternal I as the wetness of both—that quality that cannot be separate from or limited to ocean or wave, whole or part, but is the essence of both.

For those used to speaking about God as an object to be worshipped, the God of *The World Wisdom Bible* can be challenging. We are so used to identifying God with a name—Brahma, Krishna, Vishnu, Shiva, Kali, YHVH, Allah, Spirit, Mother, among others—that not having a name or seeing all names as pointing to the same reality can be more than a little unsettling. But there is no need to abandon your preferred name of God. It is not that *tathātā* is true and Krishna or Christ is false; rather, it is that Krishna and Christ and every other holy name are gateways to that which is beyond all names, even *tathātā*, and beyond naming itself.

In this way we align ourselves with the wisdom of the Hindu Rig Veda that reminded us some thirty-five hundred years ago, "Truth is one. Different people call it by different names" (1.164.46). There is no reason to abandon the name to which you have grown comfortable; simply do not imagine that Truth can be limited to one name or even all names together.

Introduction

*T*he World Wisdom Bible is rooted in one simple idea: "When you know the truth, the truth will set you free" (John 8:32). The truth we are talking about is called perennial wisdom: *perennial* because it reoccurs in every civilization throughout recorded human history, and *wisdom* because it reveals the true nature of life and how best to live it. What perennial wisdom frees you from is the illusion of otherness that fuels the sense of fear and alienation that drives so much of our ego-centered lives.

In the context of perennial wisdom and *The World Wisdom Bible*, truth is that which leads us beyond alienation and isolation to integration and unity. It is that which leads us beyond fear to love; beyond exploitation of the other to justice for all; beyond violence and war to cooperation and peace; and beyond the zero-sum, winner-takes-all worldview of "us against them" to the nonzero, win-win worldview of "all of us together." In the context of perennial wisdom and *The World Wisdom Bible*, truth is that which collapses the divisions between chosen and not chosen, believer and infidel, saved and damned, and leads to the understanding that we are all one community of seekers. Finally, in the context of perennial wisdom and *The World Wisdom Bible*, truth is that which transcends the binaries of sacred and profane, heaven and earth, Creator and creation, and allows us to cultivate an awareness wherein we may encounter every mundane, finite, nameable "this" as a manifestation of the infinite, ineffable, and divine That of which we are all a part.

While bearing the stamp of the religion and culture in which any given articulation of perennial wisdom arises, perennial wisdom can be summarized in four points:

1. All life arises in and is an expression of the non-dual Infinite Life that is called by many names: Ultimate Reality, God, Tao, Mother, Allah, YHVH, Dharmakaya, Brahma, and Great Spirit, among others.

2. You contain two ways of knowing the world: a greater knowing (called Atman, Soul, Self, Spirit, or Mind, along with a host of other names) that intuitively knows each finite life as a unique manifestation of Infinite Life, and a lesser knowing (called self, ego, *aham*, *kibr*, and the like) that mistakes uniqueness for separateness and imagines itself apart from rather than a part of Infinite Life.

3. Awakening the Self and knowing the interconnectedness of all life in the singular Life carries with it a universal ethic calling the awakened to cultivate compassion and justice toward all beings.

4. Awakening your Self and living this ethic is the highest goal you can set for yourself.

The World Wisdom Bible hopes to set you free by sharing with you many texts held sacred by the world's religions that articulate perennial wisdom. As such *The World Wisdom Bible* is a new testament for a global spirituality. By "new testament" we mean that *The World Wisdom Bible* is a contemporary anthology of ancient texts bearing witness to the universality of perennial wisdom. By "global spirituality" we mean the perennial wisdom itself, a wisdom discovered by every human community across time and tradition.

To be clear, we are not advocating a global religion, that is, a single religion to replace the many religions of humankind. We are students of comparative religion and have deep respect for both human religiosity in general and the specific religions that this innate religiosity creates. Yet we see in each specific religion a common thread that if highlighted in each faith tradition and held as a central core belief of all humans, religious and otherwise, can provide the foundation for a new civility, if not a new civilization.

The World Wisdom Bible contains many instances of perennial wisdom as it appears across a wide range of texts. While we uphold the wisdom of these texts, we do not affirm their holiness. We lift them out of their respective cultures and those belief systems that call them sacred. For us they are true, but not holy. They are true because they give voice to ideas we find intrinsically compelling and illuminating, but not holy because we make no claim regarding their divine source or sanction. Similarly, we make no claim regarding the ultimate truth or falsehood of any religion; we are only saying that we find perennial wisdom insightful and moving regardless of the religion in which we encounter it.

Boundary Crossers

Given this, let us be very clear regarding those for whom this bible was created. Our audience is not those committed to one tradition or another but rather that growing audience of spiritual boundary crossers who are open to a broader field of spiritual inquiry that embraces the entire spectrum of religion.

Readers of *The World Wisdom Bible* are—or will become—wisdom seekers who refuse to have their search for Truth limited to the truth claims of any one religion or tribe alone. Instead, they see themselves as heirs to the entirety of human wisdom. While the print edition of *The World Wisdom Bible* restricts itself—due to limits of space—to religious texts from major world religions (those typically included in studies of comparative religion and of world religious history), our website (www.worldwisdombible.org) expands our search to include not only other religious traditions but also nonreligious wisdom as well: scientific, literary, artistic, and more.

Religions Are Like Languages

Some may find it odd that while we claim to respect all religions, we reject the absolutist truth claims of every religion. If a religion is not true, why bother with it at all? The answer to this question rests with one's understanding of religion. While scholars have debated—and continue to debate—just what religion is, we take a softer approach and root our understanding of religion in the metaphor of language.

Like language, religion is a way we humans make meaning out of the raw facts of our existence. It is a human creation reflecting and shaping the civilization from which it comes. Religion, like language, is neither true nor false. It evolves over time and adapts words and concepts from other religions and languages. Religion, like language, is the way we humans archive and share experience, but it is not synonymous with experience: *d-o-g* does not bark, and *g-o-d* does not save.

Some religions, like some languages, may be better than others at expressing some things, and there may be some things you simply cannot say in a given religion or language but can say in a different religion or language. Just as being born into a mother tongue does not preclude you from speaking other languages, so being born into a specific religion or no religion at all does not preclude you from learning the wisdom of any and all religions. And just as the more languages you know the more nuanced your understanding of life becomes, so the more religions you know the more nuanced your understanding of Truth becomes.

Each Religion Speaks to a Facet of Your Experience

Taking our religion–language analogy one step further, just as each language offers its own sense of reality, so each religion offers its own sense of the human condition. And just as your sense of reality is broadened by learning multiple languages, your understanding of the human condition— your condition—is broadened by learning from the world's religions.

Borrowing from the work of Boston University professor of religion Stephen Prothero and his marvelous introduction to the world's religions, *God Is Not One: The Eight Rival Religions That Run the World*, we believe that each religion focuses on one existential problem under which humanity suffers, identifies this problem as *the* existential problem of humanity, and then sets about to solve it through the unique practices that religion contains.[1] While in no way rejecting Prothero's position, we expand it a bit.

While we agree that each religion focuses on one existential problem, we suggest that humanity suffers from all of them, though any given human may be inclined to focus on only a few or even only one. Here are the problems, presented in no particular order, proposed by the religions from which *The World Wisdom Bible* draws its texts and teachings.

Reality versus Illusion: Hinduism

According to Hinduism, the existential problem at the heart of the human condition is ignorance of the true nature of reality (*avidya*), which leaves us living in a world of illusion (*maya*). This is not to say the world itself is illusory, only that our understanding of it is.

A Hindu parable puts it this way: Imagine you awake in the middle of the night to find a poisonous snake curled at the foot of your bed. Frozen with fear, you spend the night in terror, praying that nothing will cause the snake to strike you and, in so doing, kill you. As dawn rises and sunlight floods your bedroom you realize that the "snake" is, in fact, the belt you neglected to hang up as you prepared for bed the night before. Immediately fear and terror vanish and you achieve *moksha*, liberation from the illusion of the snake and the fear and terror that the illusion elicited.

The way to liberation is through one or more of the four *yogas*: service to others (*Karma*), devotion to God (*Bhakti*); the study of wisdom (*Jnana*); and contemplative practice (*Raja*).

Alienation from God: Judaism

The existential problem that is Judaism's focus is exile (*galut*) and the alienation from God that exile entails. Humanity is meant to live in Paradise, the Garden of Eden, as tillers of the soil and midwives to nature's bounty (Genesis 2:15–16), but we were exiled from the Garden because we ate from the Tree of Knowledge of Good and Evil and fell into the trap of duality. By eating the apple, we consumed the notion that the world is a collection of opposing binaries—good versus bad, us versus them—rather than an integrated network of complementarities—front and back, good and bad, us and them, and all of us together.

The solution to this exile is returning to God (*teshuvah*) by repairing the world with godliness (*tikkun*). The means for return and repair are the 613 spiritual disciplines (*mitzvot*) of Jewish practice.

Dissatisfaction by Way of Desire: Buddhism

Buddhism sees the existential problem of humanity as a sense of deep and abiding dissatisfaction with life (*dukkha*) caused by addictive desire (*trishna*). Simply put, we want what we cannot have: permanence, immortality, surety, and security. The more we struggle to attain the unattainable, the more miserable we become and the more needless suffering we endure.

The solution to this dissatisfaction is nirvana, the cessation of addictive desire and the suffering it creates. The way to accomplish this is the Eightfold Path—right understanding of the nature of reality, right thought, right speech, right action, right livelihood, right effort, right mindfulness, and right concentration—which leads to the three essentials of Buddhist life: morality (*sila*), awakening (*samadhi*), and wisdom (*prajna*).

Stained by Sin: Christianity

According to many denominations of Christianity, the existential problem at the heart of the human condition is sin, or more specifically original sin.

The Christian insight is that there is something ontologically wrong with us, something we cannot fix on our own.

There is no discipline that will set us right. Only God can fix what is wrong, and indeed God has done so by incarnating as Jesus and dying on the cross as ransom for our sin. Within the context of Christianity—or better, the many Christianities that grow up around this idea—belief in Jesus as Christ and belief in the salvific power of his death and resurrection is the only way to get ourselves right with God.

Falling Prey to Pride: Islam

Islam identifies pride as the existential problem that most threatens human flourishing. This is because pride—following the desires of our will rather than submitting to the demands of God's will (the true meaning of *Islam*)—keeps us from living the holy life God wishes us to live.

The way of Islam is to submit ourselves to the discipline of the Five Pillars, four of which are revealed in the Hadith of Gabriel, perhaps the most important of all hadiths. (Hadiths are reports of the life of the Prophet Muhammad that Muslims consider historical and use as the basis, along with the Qur'an, for the practical and ethical ideals of Islam.)

> One day while the Prophet Muhammad (Peace Be Upon Him) was sitting in the company of others, the Angel Jibreel (Gabriel) came and asked, "What is Islam?" Muhammad replied, "To worship Allah alone and none other, to pray five times daily, to offer charity according to the law, and to fast during the month of Ramadan." (Sahih al-Bukhari 1:2:48)

To these four, add the fifth, which is mentioned in a separate hadith: making pilgrimage to Mecca at least once during our lifetime, finances permitting.

Adherence to these five pillars helps us overcome pride, place our will secondary to God's will, and live as God expects and requires.

Losing Touch with Our Heart: Confucianism

For Confucianism the existential problem we humans face is loss of *jen* and *li*. *Jen* (pronounced *ren*) translates as human heartedness: our capacity for goodness, generosity, love of neighbor, and care for society. Humans are intrinsically capable of *jen* because we are born good, but without training in the cultivation of *jen* we tend to fall into its opposite, selfishness. *Li*, ritual or propriety, is the way to live our lives and order our society to promote *jen*. *Jen* and *li* together create *junzi*, the superior person, whose actions are always proper and whose overriding concern is the welfare of others.

The way to cultivate *jen* and *li* is the Confucian system of education that focuses on the classics of Chinese literature and building moral character.

Prisoners of Formality: Taoism

The existential problem highlighted in Taoism is the loss of our intrinsic naturalness. Unlike the Confucian, who believes that our innate goodness needs to be cultivated through formal moral training and literary education, the Taoist holds that we are born free, that goodness arises naturally from living that freedom, and the constraints of formal training and education ensnare us in systems of convention that rob us of our freedom. The solution is to return to the Tao, the way of nature, and to live in harmony with it.

While the Confucian upholds the ideal of the *junzi*, the superior person, the Taoist celebrates the *zhenren*, the genuine person. To cultivate our innate authenticity, we practice "sitting and forgetting" (ego-erasing meditation, dropping the self, and resting as the Self), "fasting of the mind" (freeing oneself of -isms and ideologies), and "free and easy wandering" (ecstatic journeying in the mountains), all of which foster an alignment with the Tao, the way of nature.

Mi Problemo, Su Problemo

Ignorance, illusion, exile, alienation, dissatisfaction, sin, pride, loss of goodness, loss of naturalness and authenticity—are any of these existential problems foreign to you? While it is true that given your personal history, both nature and nurture, genetic and parental, you may see one or more of these problems as being uppermost in your life. Still, if you examine your life carefully enough, chances are you will notice they are all at play, and therefore you can learn from all these religions.

This is what spiritual boundary crossers do: they seek out the wisdom in every tradition, religious and otherwise. And this is what we suspect you do as well. *The World Wisdom Bible* is not a textbook for the study of the world's religions but rather a compendium of wisdom drawn from the world's religions. It is our hope that you will be intrigued enough by the wisdom of these texts to seek out the complete texts and read them in context of the religions from which they come. In this way you will become literate not only in the perennial wisdom of world but also in religion.

How *The World Wisdom Bible* Is Organized

The first four chapters of *The World Wisdom Bible* are organized around the four *Mahavakyas*, or Great Teachings of the Hindu Upanishads: *tat tvam asi*, God as Ultimate Reality; *aham brahmāsmi*, God as Eternal Subject; *ayam ātmā brahma*, God as awakened Self; and *prajñānam brahma*, God as Wisdom. Chapter 5 lays out the qualities of the wise, those awakened women and men who know God as All in all. Chapter 6 speaks to the Way, or spiritual path the wise follow and that you may follow as well. Chapter 7 explores the ethics that arise when you know the interrelatedness of all things in, with, and as God. Chapter 8 speaks to the way the wise die, that is, how best to surrender to the ocean who has been waving as you.

These chapters are followed by three appendices. The first, "Warnings from the Dark Side," contains texts from various scriptures dealing with war, violence, misogyny, and genocide. These are included not as ideals to be lived but as warnings to be heeded regarding acts to be avoided. The second appendix contains the Eight Points of Agreement that grew out of an interspiritual experiment conducted over three decades by Father Thomas Keating. Father Thomas sought to create a contemporary perennial wisdom community, and these eight points can help you do the same. The third appendix contains the United Nations' Universal Declaration of Human Rights, a concise, clear, and intrinsically true affirmation of a global ethic perfectly compatible with the ancient texts included in this testament. While chapter 7 spreads out many teachings on ethical living from many traditions, the Universal Declaration of Human Rights suggests how these might be used in a global rather than just a personal and interpersonal setting.

How to Use This Book

What you will find in these pages are selections from a variety of texts held sacred by one or more of the world's religions. No attempt is made to link a specific text with a specific religion or the existential problem on which that religion may focus. Nor do we provide a running commentary to each text to guide your reading in order that you come to the same conclusion regarding it as we do. Rather we jumble the texts together as if they were variations on a theme—which we believe they are—and leave it up to you to discover the wisdom within them.

By juxtaposing these texts, we invite them to dialogue with one another, and by not providing you with an interpretive guide, we invite you to dialogue with them as well. The Truth is not in the texts but in your encounter with the texts. The more you read them, the more insight you will glean, but your reading will always be distinctly yours.

When reading *The World Wisdom Bible*, do not ask what these texts mean in the context of their respective religions; rather, ask what these texts mean in the context of your life. We want you to ask how the wisdom of these texts can liberate you from the parochial for the universal, from the zero-sum worldview you may have been taught for the nonzero worldview these wisdom teachings promote. This bible invites you to join in an ancient and ongoing conversation with Truth, a discussion in which we hope you will choose to engage with an open mind, an open heart, and open arms.

The World Wisdom Bible is a resource to be tapped and not necessarily a book to be read cover to cover or in any specific sequence. Our hope is that you will turn to it for insight and wisdom and to broaden your sense of what is true beyond the boundaries of fixed religious traditions. As such, this is a book that belongs on your nightstand rather than your bookshelf.

CHAPTER ONE

Ultimate Reality

Recognizing the One That Is All

When we speak of God as Absolute or Ultimate Reality, we are not speaking of the Tao that can be named. Nor are we speaking of the God of any theology or religion. Rather, we mean the eternal and unnameable Tao, the reality beyond all theologies and systems of belief. While it is commonplace to think of God as a being or even a supreme being, Ultimate Reality is *being* itself: not a noun, but a verb; not a person, but a process; not YHVH, Allah, Jesus, Brahma, Vishnu, Shiva, or any other of the named Gods of human history, but that toward which these names point when they are used to articulate perennial wisdom rather than a parochial theology.

While Ultimate Reality cannot be reduced to words, it can be hinted at by the classic symbol of the Tao, yin and yang:

This symbol represents all life as the dynamic flow of complementarities: yin goes with yang the way up goes with down, good goes with evil, back goes with front, and heads goes with tails. While each side is distinct from the other, you cannot have one without the other, and both are expressions of a greater wholeness. It is that wholeness that we term the unnameable Tao, the greater wholeness that is Ultimate Reality.

In the teachings that follow, you will find texts using many names to point toward the Nameless. While in the context of the religions from which these teachings come one name may be valued above others, in the context of the perennial wisdom of *The World Wisdom Bible* they are all synonyms for that which cannot be named.

As the spider moves along the thread,
as small sparks come forth from the fire,
even so from this Self [*Brahma*]
come forth all breaths, all worlds,
all divinities, all beings.
　　(Brihadaranyaka Upanishad 2.1.20)

YHVH is One in all the worlds and the entire creation,
an absolutely simple Oneness,
and all things are reduced to nothing,
and there is nothing but YHVH at all.
　　(Rabbi Chaim of Volozhin, *Nefesh HaChayim*, *Sha'ar Gimmel*, *Perek* 6)

The whole world is pervaded by Me,
yet my form is not seen.
All living things have their being in Me,
yet I am not limited by them.
　　(Bhagavad Gita 9:4; Shri Purohit Swami, trans., *Bhagavad Gita: Annotated & Explained*, p. 71)

God is Light.
　　(1 John 1:5)

Even the material earth,
appearing to the eye of each to be truly existent,
is naught and actual nothingness with respect to the Holy One.

> (Rabbi Schneur Zalman of Liady, *Sha'ar HaYichud veHaEmunah*, *Perek* 6)

With respect to the Holy One,
there is nothing into which the One could expand
because there is nothing other than the One itself.

> (Rabbi Aharon HaLevi Horowitz, *Sha'arei HaYichud veHaEmunah*, *Sha'ar* 1,
> *Perek* 24, *Daf* 49a)

This one Thing, breathless,
breathed by its own nature—
apart from this nothing whatsoever exists.
From this arose the primal seed and germ of spirit.

> (Rig Veda 10.129)

Above and below, in heaven and on earth,
everything is absolutely empty and without substance—
although this is impossible to explain,
it can be grasped according to the intuition of each person.

> (Rabbi Noson, *Likkutei Halakhos*, *Matnas Sh'chiv me-Ra'* 2:2)

Know this day and take it to heart
that YHVH is God,
in the heavens above
and on earth below;
there is nothing else.

> (Deuteronomy 4:39)

That which cannot be articulated
but from which all speech comes, that alone is Brahma.
That which mind cannot understand
but by which the mind is understood, that alone is Brahma.
That which the eye cannot see
but by which the eye is seen, that alone is Brahma.
That which the ear cannot hear
but by which the ear hears, that alone is Brahma.
　　(Kena Upanishad 1.5–8)

YHVH is One, creating all;
YHVH is all.
　　(Rabbi Abraham ibn Ezra, *Perush* on *B'reishit* 1:26)

Those who join themselves to God
are of the same spirit as God.
　　(1 Corinthians 6:17)

God is found in all things
and all things are found in God.
Everything is in God,
and God is in everything and beyond everything,
and there is nothing beside God.
　　(Rabbi Moshe Cordovero, *Sefer Elimah*, *Daf* 24b)

All the Buddhas and all sentient beings are
nothing but the One Mind,
beside which nothing exists.
This Mind, which is without beginning,

is unborn and indestructible.

It transcends all limits, measures, names,

traces, and comparisons.

Only awake to the One mind.

> (Huang Po; John Blofeld, trans., *The Zen Teaching of Huang Po*, pp. 29–30)

Everything is God who makes everything be,

and in truth

the world of seemingly separate entities

is entirely annulled.

> (Rabbi Schneur Zalman of Liady, *Likkutei Torah, Shir HaShirim* 41a)

Truly, God is the One

who splits the grain and the kernel apart,

bringing forth the living from the dead,

and God is the One who brings forth the dead

out of that which is alive.

> (Qur'an 6:95; Camille Helminski, trans., *The Light of Dawn: Daily Readings from the Holy Qur'an*, p. 26)

As sparks of flame by the thousands

issue from a blazing fire,

so all beings issue from and return to

the Immutable One.

> (Mundaka Upanishad 2.1.1)

Just as You are in me, and I am in You,

may they be one in Us.

> (John 17:21)

The essence of divinity is found in every single thing—
nothing but This exists.
Do not attribute duality to God.
Do not say, "This is a stone and not God."
Rather, all existence is God,
and the stone is a thing pervaded by divinity.
(*Shi'ur Qomah* to *Zohar* 3:14b, *Idra Rabba*)

Look at it, it cannot be seen
It is called colorless
Listen to it, it cannot be heard
It is called noiseless
Reach for it, it cannot be held
It is called formless
These three cannot be completely unraveled
So they are combined into one
Above it, not bright
Below it, not dark
Continuing endlessly, cannot be named
It returns back into nothingness
Thus it is called the form of the formless
The image of the imageless
This is called enigmatic
Confront it, its front cannot be seen
Follow it, its back cannot be seen
Wield the Tao of the ancients
To manage the existence of today
One can know the ancient beginning
It is called the Tao Axiom
(Tao Te Ching 14; Derek Lin, trans., *Tao Te Ching: Annotated & Explained*,
p. 29)

The One is without boundaries
Nothing exists outside of it to border it

The One cannot be investigated
Nothing exists apart from it to investigate it
The One cannot be measured
Nothing exists external to it to measure it
The One cannot be seen for no one can envision it
The One is eternal for it exists forever
The One is inconceivable for no one can comprehend it
The One is indescribable for no one can put any words to it.

> (Secret Book of John; Steven Davies, trans., *The Secret Book of John: The Gnostic Gospel—Annotated & Explained*, p. 13)

Where can I go from Your Spirit?
Where can I flee from Your presence?
If I ascend to the heavens, You are there;
if I make my bed in the depths, You are there.
If I rise in the East with the dawn,
if I settle in the West with dusk,
even there Your hand will guide me,
Your right hand will hold me fast.
If I say, "Surely the darkness will shroud me,"
the night would become as light around me.
For darkness is not dark to You;
and night no less revealing than day,
for darkness and light are the same to You.

> (Psalm 139:7–12)

One and Infinite,
beyond north and south,
east and west,
above and below.
One who knows this
becomes this.

> (Maitri Upanishad 6.17)

What is meant by non-duality?
It means the light and dark,
long and short, black and white,
are not independent of one another.
Even nirvana and samsara, the Absolute and the Relative,
are not two but one,
for there can be no Absolute without Relative
and no Relative without Absolute.
Therefore it can be said that all things are non-dual,
and each thing is part of all things.
  (Lankavatara Sutra 136)

To God belong the east and the west.
Wherever you turn, there is the face of God.
Witness, God is infinite, all-knowing.
  (Qur'an 2:115; Camille Helminski, trans., *The Light of Dawn:
  Daily Readings from the Holy Qur'an*, p. 3)

Where I wander—You!
Where I wonder—You!
Only You, You again, You always!
You! You! You!
When I am happy—You!
When I am sad—You!
Only You, You again, You always!
You! You! You!
Sky—You!
Earth—You!
You above!
You below!
In the beginning—You!
In the end—You!

Only You, You again, You always!
You! You! You!

> (Rabbi Levi Yitzchak of Berditchev; *Hasidic Tales: Annotated & Explained*,
> p. 177)

There was something formlessly created
Born before Heaven and Earth.
So silent! So ethereal!
Independent and changeless
Circulating and ceaseless
It may be regarded as the mother of the world
I do not know its name
Identifying it, I call it Tao

> (Tao Te Ching 25; Derek Lin, trans., *Tao Te Ching: Annotated & Explained*,
> p. 51)

God—there is no god but God!
To God belongs what is in the heavens
and what is on earth.

> (Qur'an 2:255; Yusuf Ali, trans., revised by Sohaib N. Sultan, *The Qur'an
> and Sayings of the Prophet Muhammad: Selections Annotated & Explained*,
> p. 17)

All things have a "this" and a "that."
Looking at them only from the perspective of "this,"
we can't really see them for what they are,
and only by knowing them as they really are
can we understand them.
Realize: all "this" arises from "that,"
and all "that" follows "this."
"This" and "that" are interdependent and co-originating:
as one arises, the other ends,
and as one ends, the other arises;

as one is acceptable,
the other becomes unacceptable,
and as one is unacceptable,
the other becomes acceptable.
Thus, "this" and "that" are intimately connected,
and "right" and "wrong" depend on each other.

> (Chuang-tzu 2; Livia Kohn, trans., *Chuang-tzu: The Tao of Perfect Happiness—Annotated & Explained*, p. 127)

God is that in whom we live
and move
and have our being.

> (Acts 17:28)

The essence of God is kindness,
and all that is kind is God.
God is nature's father and mother,
her source and substance.

> (Julian of Norwich, *Revelations of Divine Love*, 62)

The Tao that can be spoken is not the eternal Tao
The name that can be named is not the eternal name
The nameless is the origin of Heaven and Earth
The named is the mother of myriad things
Thus, constantly without desire, one observes its essence
Constantly with desire, one observes its manifestations
These two emerge together but differ in name
The unity is said to be the mystery
Mystery of mysteries, the door to all wonders

> (Tao Te Ching 1; Derek Lin, trans., *Tao Te Ching: Annotated & Explained*, p. 3)

Words are not Ultimate Truth
and what can be articulated in words is not the Ultimate Truth.
Truth is the non-dual Reality inwardly realized by the wise,
and does not fit in the world of words.
The world is nothing but Mind. All is mind.

    (Lankavatara Sutra)

God alone can be called "mother,"
for only God is so loving, kind, wise, knowing, and good.
While your body when compared with your soul may appear lesser,
it is no less the doing of God,
who knows your needs,
and watching you grow
attends to your changing conditions as any mother would.

    (Julian of Norwich, *Revelations of Divine Love*, 60)

You are the All in all,
and everything is in You.
You are what is,
and there is nothing else but You.

    (Acts of Peter 39)

The Tao is empty
When utilized, it is not filled up
So deep! It seems to be the source of all things
It blunts the sharpness
Unravels the knots
Dims the glare
Mixes the dusts
So indistinct! It seems to exist
I do not know whose offspring it is
Its image is the predecessor of God

    (Tao Te Ching 4; Derek Lin, trans., *Tao Te Ching: Annotated & Explained*, p. 9)

The Living Light therefore speaks
with the secret word of Wisdom:
God is full and whole and beyond the beginning of time,
and therefore God cannot be divided or analyzed
by words as a human being can.
God is a whole and nothing other than a whole,
to which nothing can be added
and from which nothing can be taken away.
For God-who-is is both paternity and divinity,
since it is said, "I am who I am."
And God-who-is is fullness itself.
How is this to be understood?
By God's activity, creativity, and perfection.

> (Hildegard of Bingen, "To Odo of Soissons, 1148"; *Epistolarium* [Letters] 39R; Sheryl Kujawa-Holbrook, trans., *Hildegard of Bingen: Essential Writings and Chants of a Christian Mystic—Annotated & Explained*, p. 51)

Universal Mind exists like a vast and boundless ocean.
Waves disturb its surface, but beneath,
all is calm and eternally unmoved.
Having no personality, all things are in it.
But due to the disturbance upon its surface
it became an actor playing many parts.

> (Lankavatara Sutra)

The One is the Invisible Spirit.
It is not right to think of it as a God
Or as like God.
It is more than just God.
Nothing is above it. Nothing rules it.

Since everything exists within it
It does not exist within anything.

> (Secret Book of John; Stevan Davies, trans., *The Secret Book of John: The Gnostic Gospel—Annotated & Explained*, p. 11)

All that is manifest is filled with God.
All that is unmanifest is filled with God.
From God all things flow.
All things come from God,
yet God alone does not change.

> (Isha Upanishad 1)

Truth is one.
Different people call it by different names.

> (Rig Veda 1.164.46)

All living creatures born of every class,
whether from eggs or from wombs or from water,
with form or without form,
whether free or not free from thought,
or beyond the worlds of thought—
such things come from Me
so that nirvana might be attained.

> (Diamond Sutra 3)

In the beginning You laid the foundations of the earth,
and the heavens are the work of Your hands.
They will perish, but You remain;
they will all wear out like a garment.
Like clothing You will change them
and they will be discarded.

But You remain the same,
and Your years will never end.
(Psalm 102:26–28)

Not "perfect"
Not "blessed"
Not "divine"
But superior to such concepts.
Neither physical nor unphysical
Neither immense nor infinitesimal
It is impossible to specify in quantity or quality
For it is beyond knowledge.
(Secret Book of John; Stevan Davies, trans., *The Secret Book of John: The
Gnostic Gospel—Annotated & Explained*, p. 15)

As the wind, though one, takes on myriad forms,
so too the Spirit.
There is only this One,
inside and outside,
transforming into the many.
(Katha Upanishad 2.2.12)

Light producing light.
Life producing life
Blessedness producing blessedness
Knowledge producing knowledge
Good producing goodness
Mercy producing mercy
Generosity producing generosity
It does not "possess" these things.
(Secret Book of John; Stevan Davies, trans., *The Secret Book of John: The
Gnostic Gospel—Annotated & Explained*, pp. 17, 19)

All life, mind, and sense
come from the One.
All space, light, air, fire, and water
come from the One.
Indeed from the One comes all.
   (Mundaka Upanishad 3.1)

I form light.
I create darkness.
I bring good.
I create evil.
I, YHVH, do all things.
   (Isaiah 45:7)

The glory of God pervades the universe.
God moves and is still,
God is near and far.
God is within all and outside all.
   (Isha Upanishad 1.5)

God's only desire is
to reveal unity through diversity.
That is, to reveal that
all of reality is unique
and yet united in a fundamental oneness.
   (Rabbi Aharon HaLevi Horowitz, *Sha'arei HaYichud veHaEmunah*, *Perek* 4,
   Daf 5)

Beyond the senses is the brain.
Beyond the brain is the intellect.
Beyond the intellect is the Self.
Beyond the Self is the Unmanifest God.
Beyond God is the I
All-pervading Subject impossible to objectify.
  (Katha Upanishad 2.3.7–8)

God causes the sun to shine
on the evil as well as the good,
and sends rainfall upon the just as well as the unjust.
  (Matthew 5:45)

Rain falls on both the just and the unjust.
  (Babylonian Talmud, *Taanit* 7a)

Whoever sees me (Jesus) sees God.
  (John 14:9)

Whoever sees me [Muhammad] sees Truth.
  (Hadith of Bukhari 87:15)

CHAPTER TWO

The Eternal I

Understanding God-Consciousness

Returning once again to our analogy of ocean and wave, with Ultimate Reality as the infinite ocean and the Self or Mind as the awakened wave, we can say that the Eternal I is the wetness of both. While we can imagine the difference between ocean and wave, the one being the whole of which the other is a part, we cannot imagine wetness. While we can speak of the ocean as greater than the sum of its waves, we cannot speak of wetness as greater than the ocean or the wave but rather the essence of both. Wetness is the very isness of ocean and wave. In this way the Eternal I is the very isness—or better, I-ness—of Ultimate Reality and Self.

The Eternal I is awake to both Ultimate Reality and Self. The Eternal I is Jesus, who says, "I and the Father are one" (John 10:30); and YHVH, who says, "I form light and create darkness, I fashion good and create evil; I, YHVH, do all things" (Isaiah 45:7); and the ninth-century Sufi saint Mansur al-Hallaj, who says, "I am the Truth"; and Krishna, who says, "I am the source of all; from Me everything flows" (Bhagavad Gita 10:8). You too are the Eternal I, but because the Eternal I is pure Subject and you are conditioned to think of God as absolute object, you are mostly ignorant of the Eternal I as your essence.

There is an Indian story of ten fools who ford a stream together. When they arrive on the far shore they each count the others to make sure they all made it safely across. Forgetting to include themselves, however, they continually come up one person short, but since each is accounted for in the others' counting, they cannot figure out who among them is missing.

The nineteenth-century Jewish sage Chanoch Henich tells a similar story:

> There was once a fellow who was very forgetful. Indeed, his memory was so short that when he awoke each morning he could not remember where he had laid his clothes the night before. Things got so bad for him that he could not fall asleep, so great was his nervousness about finding his things upon waking.
>
> One evening, however, he hit on a great idea. Taking pencil and paper, he wrote down exactly where he had placed each item of clothing. Placing his notes on the nightstand by his bed, he quickly fell asleep, confident that he would find everything just perfectly in the morning. And indeed he did. He woke up, took the notes from his nightstand, and read off each item in turn: "Pants—on chair back"; and there they were. He put them on. "Shirt—on bed post"; and there it was. He put it on. "Hat—on desk"; and there it sat. He placed it on his head. In a few minutes the fellow was completely dressed. But suddenly a great dread came upon him.
>
> "Yes, yes," he said aloud. "Here are my pants, my shirt, and my cap; but where am I?"
>
> He looked and looked and looked, but he could find himself nowhere.[1]

Reb Chanoch would pause after each telling of this tale and then conclude saying, "And that is how it is with each of us as well."[2]

Read as parables rather than as jokes, the "missing" one in both stories is the Eternal I that cannot be counted because it is always; it is only subject and never object. Forgetting that we are each this Eternal I is "how it is with each of us," and because this is how it is with each of us, we all suffer from a case of mistaken identity, imagining we are other than the One that is all.

Zen people have a koan, "Show me your face before your parents were born." A koan is a puzzle that cannot be solved logically. It has to be embodied and lived from the inside out rather than tackled from the outside in. You become the koan rather than solve the koan. To show your face before your parents were born is to drop the face you have at the moment—to drop the egoic I conditioned and defined by the narratives of religion, nationality, ethnicity, gender, and culture and realize the Eternal I who has no narrative and cannot be conditioned or defined.

Notice there is no *becoming* the Eternal I. There is no transition from egoic I to Eternal I, only a spontaneous realization that the singular Eternal I is you at this and every moment. The Eternal I is Ultimate Reality and awakened Self experienced from the inside out. It is not male or female; it is not Muslim, Christian, Jewish, Buddhist, Hindu, or atheist; it is not liberal or conservative; it is not identified with any race, ethnicity, or nationality. It is the Knower that cannot in and of itself be known, the Seer that cannot in and of itself be seen; the Subject that cannot be turned into an object.

The challenge when reading the following texts is to read them as if you, your Self, were saying them. While the text may identify the speaker as someone in particular, know that the I of the speaker is your I, and the someone speaking is simply the only One there is.

I am the first and I am the last;
apart from me there is no God.
   (Isaiah 44:6)

I am the Alpha and the Omega,
the First and the Last,
the Beginning and the End.
   (Revelation 22:13)

God is the First and the Last,
the Manifest and the Hidden,
and [God] knows completely all things.
   (Qur'an 57:3; Camille Helminski, trans., *The Light of Dawn: Daily Readings from the Holy Qur'an*, p. 161)

Know this and see what is so:
I am God.
I am everything.
I am every happening.
I am the endless shaping of creation,
and I am the conclusion to which all action leads.
I ordained this from the moment before time.
With wisdom and love all things happen;
there can be no errors.

(Julian of Norwich, *Revelations of Divine Love*, 11)

I am the Lord God of all.
I am the imperishable Source of all being.
[I am] the One, the Manifold, the Omnipresent, the Universal.
I am the Oblation, the Sacrifice, and the Worship;
I am the Fuel and the Chant,
I am the Butter offered to the fire, I am the Fire itself;
and I am the Act of offering.
I am the Father of the universe and its Mother;
I am its Nourisher and its Grandfather;
I am the Knowable and the Pure;
I am Om; and I am the Sacred Scriptures.
I am the Goal, the Sustainer, the Lord,
the Witness, the Home, the Shelter,
the Lover, and the Origin;
I am Life and Death;
I am the Fountain and the Seed Imperishable.
I am the Heat of the Sun.
I release and hold back the Rains.
I am Death and Immortality;
I am Being and Not-Being.

(Bhagavad Gita 9:11, 13, 15, 16, 17, 18, 19; Shri Purohit Swami, trans.,
Bhagavad Gita: Annotated and Explained, p. 73)

I fill the hearts of those who love me,

they will never lack for insight.

I am the deep grain of creation, the subtle current of life.

God fashioned me before all things;

I am the blueprint of creation.

I was there from the beginning, from before there was a beginning.

I am independent of time and space, earth and sky.

I was before depth was conceived,

before springs bubbled with water,

before the shaping of mountains and hills,

before God fashioned the earth and its bounty,

before the first dust settled on the land.

When God prepared the heavens, I was there.

When the circle of the earth was etched into the face of the deep,

I was there.

When the stars and planets soared into their orbit,

when the deepest oceans found their level

and the dry land established the shores,

I was there.

I stood beside God as firstborn and friend.

My nature is joy, and I gave God constant delight.

Now that the world is inhabited, I rejoice in it.

I will be your true delight if you will heed my teachings.

(Proverbs 8:21–31; *Proverbs: Annotated & Explained*, p. 55)

I am the Self, seated in the hearts of all beings;

I am the beginning and the life,

and I am the end of them all.

I am Nature;

I am the Mind;

I am the Intelligence in all that lives.

I am the Life;

I am the Energy in fire, earth, wind, sky, heaven, sun, moon, and
planets.
I am Death.
I am the Eternal Present;
I am the Beginning, the Middle, and the End in creation;
I am Time inexhaustible;
and I am the all-pervading Preserver.
I am all-devouring Death;
I am the Origin of all that shall happen;
I am Fame, Fortune, Speech, Memory, Intellect, Constancy, and
Forgiveness.
I am the Silence of mystery and the Wisdom of the wise.
I am the Seed of all being.
No creature moving or unmoving can live without Me.
I sustain this universe with only a small part of Myself.

    (Bhagavad Gita 10:20, 22, 23, 29, 30, 32, 33, 34, 38, 39, 42; Shri Purohit
    Swami, trans., *Bhagavad Gita: Annotated and Explained*, pp. 81, 83, 85)

I am the bread of life.
I am the light of the world.
I am before Abraham was.
I am the gate.
I am the good shepherd.
I am the resurrection and the life.
I am the way, the truth, and the life.
I am the true vine.

    (John 6:35, 8:12, 8:58, 10:9, 10:11, 11:25, 14:6, 15:1)

I am the light above everything.
I am everything.
Everything came forth from me, and everything reached me.
Split wood, I am there.
Lift up a rock, you will find me there.

    (Gospel of Thomas 77a–b; Stevan Davies, trans., *The Gospel of Thomas:
    Annotated & Explained*, p. 99)

I am with you always.
I am the Father.
The Mother.
The Son.
I am the incorruptible.

> (Secret Book of John; Stevan Davies, trans., *The Secret Book of John:
> Annotated & Explained*, p. 9)

I am you, and you are Me,
and where you are, there I am.
I am sown in all things,
and when you gather me it is you, yourself, whom you gather.

> (Gospel of Eve; *Panarion* 26.3.1)

The Ineffable says:
Understand that I am God;
there is no god before Me or any after Me.
I alone am the One Who Is,
and there is no one else to save you.

> (Isaiah 43:10–11, 44:6)

The Ineffable says:
I am the One Who Is;
there is nothing else.
Beside Me, there is no god.

> (Isaiah 45:5)

I bake my bread
and prepare my mind
within.
(The Thunder, Perfect Mind)

I am with you.
My breath is always within you.
Fear not!
(Haggai 1:13, 2:5)

I am Brahma.
(Brihadaranyaka Upanishad 1.4.10)

I am found in those who seek Me.
See Me. Consider Me. Hear Me,
you who have ears to hear.
(The Thunder, Perfect Mind)

I am the one whose image is great.
I am the one without image at all.
I am the one hated everywhere.
I am the one lived everywhere.
I am the one who is called Life
and yet you call death.
I am the one who is called Order
and yet you call chaos.
I am the one you have sought.
I am the one you have found.
I am She without festivals
and I am She with numerous festivals.
(The Thunder, Perfect Mind)

I am the eternal and the transient.
I am the one, and the many.
  (The Thunder, Perfect Mind)

I have come to teach you
About what is, and what was, and what will be
In order for you to understand
The invisible world, and the world that is visible
And the immovable race of perfect humanity.
  (Secret Book of John; Stevan Davies, trans., *The Secret Book of John:
  Annotated & Explained*, p. 9)

I bring the clear light of unity
to those suffering from the delusion of duality.
If you can fathom my true nature,
you will behold and know your true nature as well.
  (Dharmakaya Sutra 4.26)

Where two or three gather in my name,
I am with them.
  (Matthew 18:20)

When two sit together and share words of Wisdom,
the Divine rests between them.
  (*Pirke Avot* 3:3; *Ethics of the Sages: Pirke Avot—Annotated & Explained*, p. 39)

I am the first thought that dwells in the light.
I am the movement that dwells in the All.

I am She in whom the All manifests.
I am the invisible and the revealed.
I cannot be measured.
No words can describe me.
Yet I can be known with the silence
of the One I move in all things.
    (Trimorphic Protennoia)

I can be heard in everything.
I am the speech that cannot be grasped.
I alone exist.
    (The Thunder, Perfect Mind)

I am the perfect thought of the Invisible One,
through Me the all became manifest.
I am the Mother and the Light.
    (Trimorphic Protennoia)

I am the beginning and the end.
I am the one who is honored and the one who is disposed.
I am the holy one and the whore.
I am the virgin and the wife.
I am the one with children
and They are many.
    (The Thunder, Perfect Mind)

Am I God only to those nearby,
and not those far away?
If you go into hiding,
do I not see you?
I embrace heaven and earth.

I have heard the false prophets prophesy in My name, saying,
"I had a dream! I had a dream!"
They dream only of their own deceitful desire,
and hope to make you forget My Name
in favor of their dreams.
The one with My word speaks truth.
My word is like fire, like a hammer shattering rock.

> (Jeremiah 23:23–29; *The Hebrew Prophets: Selections Annotated & Explained*,
> p. 65)

CHAPTER THREE

The Self or Mind

Awakening to Your Divine Nature

As we stated in "A Note on God," one way to think about Ultimate Reality is as an infinite ocean, and one way to understand the Self—or as the Buddhists call it, Mind—is as a wave of the ocean that has awakened to both its infinite oceanic nature and its finite wave nature. Just as Ultimate Reality is you, so you are the Self, especially the innate capacity of the Self or Mind. As the English poet William Blake puts it in *Auguries of Innocence*:

> To see a World in a Grain of Sand
> And a Heaven in a Wild Flower
> Hold Infinity in the palm of your hand
> And Eternity in an hour."[1]

This Self is operating at each moment, though so distracted are we by our particular wave that we rarely register the wisdom the Self proclaims, what Vietnamese Zen master Thich Nhat Hanh calls interbeing.

> If you are a poet, you will see clearly that there is a cloud floating in this sheet of paper. Without a cloud, there will be no rain; without rain, the trees cannot grow: and without trees, we cannot make paper. The cloud is essential for the paper to exist. If the cloud is not here, the sheet of paper cannot be here either. So we can say that the cloud and the paper inter-are....

If we look into this sheet of paper even more deeply, we can see the sunshine in it. If the sunshine is not there, the forest cannot grow. In fact nothing can grow. Even we cannot grow without sunshine. And so, we know that the sunshine is also in this sheet of paper. The paper and the sunshine inter-are. And if we continue to look we can see the logger who cut the tree and brought it to the mill to be transformed into paper. And we see the wheat. We know that the logger cannot exist without his daily bread, and therefore the wheat that became his bread is also in this sheet of paper. And the logger's father and mother are in it too. When we look in this way we see that without all of these things, this sheet of paper cannot exist.[2]

The Self is you, just as Ultimate Reality is you: not the egoic you that is defined by sex, gender, race, ethnicity, religion, politics, or nationality, but the truest you unfettered by -isms and ideologies; the you that knows the interbeing of all beings in the greater *being* of Ultimate Reality. This can be difficult to grasp because we are habituated to seeing ourselves as separate from other selves, and of imagining God to be something else altogether. But from the point of view of perennial wisdom, there is no something else—only God.

When you understand yourselves
you will be understood.
And you will realize that you are children of the living God.
If you do not know yourselves,
then you exist in poverty and
you are that poverty.

> (Gospel of Thomas 3b; Stevan Davies, trans., *The Gospel of Thomas: Annotated & Explained*, p. 5)

When you see all beings in the Self
and the Self in all beings
you fear no one.

> (Isha Upanishad 6)

Jesus said:

Blessed is one who existed

before coming into being.

> (Gospel of Thomas 19a; Stevan Davies, trans., *The Gospel of Thomas: Annotated & Explained*, p. 27)

Truth shines as itself

in your imageless mind.

It is a self-sustaining light,

and whoever partakes of it

does so only in the imageless mind,

allowing you to see beyond

the delusion and fog of temporary mind.

> (Dharmakaya Sutra 4.12)

Jesus said:

If they ask you, "Where are you from?"

reply to them,

"We have come from the place

where light is produced from itself.

It came and revealed itself in their image."

If they ask you, "Are you it?"

reply to them,

"We are its children.

"We are chosen ones of the living God."

If they ask you,

"What is the sign within you of your God?"

reply to them,

"It is movement. It is rest."

> (Gospel of Thomas 50a–c; Stevan Davies, trans., *The Gospel of Thomas: Annotated & Explained*, p. 65)

You are That.

(Chandogya Upanishad 6.8.7)

Salome asked him:
Who are you, man?
As though coming from someone,
you have come onto my couch and eaten from my table.
Jesus replied:
I am one who comes into being
from One who is the same.
Some of the things of the One have been given to me.
[Salome said:]
I am your disciple.
Therefore I say that if one is unified one will be filled with light,
but if one is divided one will be filled with darkness.

(Gospel of Thomas 61b–c; Stevan Davies, trans., *The Gospel of Thomas: Annotated & Explained*, p. 81)

True perfection is real and is found only in the real.
It is the contentless awareness of your unborn mind
shining before the dualism of temporary mind.

(Dharmakaya Sutra 4.16)

Jesus said:
You who knows everything else
but who does not know yourself
knows nothing.

(Gospel of Thomas 67; Stevan Davies, trans., *The Gospel of Thomas: Annotated & Explained*, p. 89)

The Self is Brahma.

> (Brihadaranyaka Upanishad 4.4.5)

Jesus said:

When you give rise to that which is within you,

what you have will save you.

If you do not give rise to it,

what you do not have will destroy you.

> (Gospel of Thomas 70; Stevan Davies, trans., *The Gospel of Thomas: Annotated & Explained*, p. 93)

There is nothing closer to you than God,

not even your own soul.

For God is that in which your soul rests,

through which it draws strength,

and from which it learns love.

God unites body and soul

for both find their foundation in God.

> (Julian of Norwich, *Revelations of Divine Love*, 56)

You saw Spirit and became Spirit.

You saw Christ and you became Christ.

You saw the father and you shall become the father.

Thus, in this world you indeed see everything

and do not see yourself, but in that other place

you do see yourself—and you shall become what you see.

> (Gospel of Philip, 38; Andrew Phillip Smith, trans., *The Gospel of Philip: Annotated & Explained*, p. 45)

Whoever would tend me, should tend the sick.

> (Vinaya, Mahavagga 8.26.3)

Just as you do to the least among you,
you do to me.
   (Matthew 25:40)

You cannot see That which is the Seer.
You cannot hear That which is the Hearer.
You cannot think That which is the Thinker.
You cannot know That which is the Knower.
This is your Self,
that is within all;
everything but This is transient.
   (Brihadaranyaka Upanishad 3.4.2)

Both the self and the absence of self are taught.
Also neither self nor absence of self is taught.
Everything is either real or unreal,
or both real and unreal
or neither not real nor real—
this is the teaching of the Buddha.
   (Nargajuna, Mulamadhyamikakarika)

Becoming one with your unborn mind
is to be immersed in undivided awareness
and free from the illusion of dualistic seeing.
Being immersed in undivided awareness
is the very truth of nirvana.
   (Dharmakaya Sutra 4.23)

CHAPTER FOUR

The Nature of Wisdom

Overcoming the Illusion of Separateness

In a private letter to Robert S. Marcus on the occasion of the death of Mr. Marcus's son, Albert Einstein wrote:

> A human being is a part of the whole, called by us "Universe," a part limited in time and space. He experiences himself, his thoughts and feelings as something separated from the rest—a kind of optical delusion of his consciousness. The striving to free oneself from this delusion is the one issue of true religion. Not to nourish the delusion but to try to overcome it is the way to reach the attainable measure of peace of mind.[1]

Einstein's "true religion" lifts us beyond the delusion of a separate self to the realization of the singular and infinite Self, also experienced as Ultimate Reality and the Eternal I. The capacity to see through the optical delusion and know yourself to be part of the infinite Self, the Eternal I of Ultimate Reality, is what we are calling wisdom. Realizing and living from this wisdom is the goal of "true religion."

Wisdom here is not Hindu, Jewish, Buddhist, Taoist, Confucian, Christian, or Muslim but wisdom itself: the realization that all things are manifestations of the one and only thing, called by and yet never limited to many names—God, Tao, Brahma, Allah, YHVH, Nature, Mother, and more.

In this chapter, Wisdom, which is personified here as female, speaks for herself in the first person, is spoken to in the second person, and is spoken about in the third person. In all cases the message of Wisdom is the same: each and all are one.

Who knows the root of Wisdom?
Who fathoms Her subtleties?
There is only one so wise and so wondrous—God.
God created Her and saw Her true nature.
God gave Her life and poured Her out upon all creation.
She is with you according to your ability to know Her
for God has given Her to all who love the Divine.
　　(Sirach 1:6–10)

I am the Mother of true love,
wonder, knowledge, and holy hope.
Beyond time, I am yet given to time,
a gift to all My children:
to all that God has named.
　　(Sirach 24:18)

What is Wisdom?
She is intelligent, holy, unique,
subtle, flowing, transparent, and pure;
She is distinct, invulnerable, good,
keen, irresistible, and gracious;
She is humane, faithful, sure, calm,
all-powerful, all-seeing, and available to all
who are intelligent, pure, and altogether simple.
　　(Wisdom of Solomon 7:22–23; *The Divine Feminine in Biblical Wisdom Literature:*
　　Selections Annotated & Explained, p. 29)

[Wisdom] is the mobility of movement;

She is the transparent nothing that pervades all things.

She is the breath of God,

a clear emanation of Divine Glory.

No impurity can stain Her.

She is God's spotless mirror reflecting eternal light,

and the image of divine goodness.

> (Wisdom of Solomon 7:24–26; *The Divine Feminine in Biblical Wisdom Literature: Selections Annotated & Explained*, p. 31)

Although She is one,

She does all things.

Without leaving Herself

She renews all things.

Generation after generation She slips into holy souls,

making them friends of God, and prophets;

for God loves none more than they who dwell with Wisdom.

> (Wisdom of Solomon 7:27–28; *The Divine Feminine in Biblical Wisdom Literature: Selections Annotated & Explained*, p. 33)

When Wisdom is embraced

righteousness, justice, and fairness are known;

all paths are illumined and you need fear no detour.

When Wisdom enters your heart and knowledge your soul,

you will perceive the order of the universe and never despair.

You will be rescued from your own dark inclinations,

and not even the cleverest lies will deceive you.

> (Proverbs 2:9–13; *Proverbs: Annotated & Explained*, p. 13)

Wisdom's house rests on many pillars.

It is magnificent and easy to find.

Inside, She has cooked a fine meal

and sweetened Her wine with water.

Her table is set.
She sends maidens to the tallest towers to summon you.
To the simple they call:
Come, enter here.
To those who lack understanding they say:
Come, eat my food, drink My wine.
Abandon your empty life,
and walk in the way of understanding.
    (Proverbs 9:1–6; *Proverbs: Annotated & Explained*, p. 59)

When I'm with those who are spiritually mature,
I do talk about wisdom.
But this is not a worldly wisdom,
a wisdom that our political leaders could understand;
their kind of wisdom is leading them to destruction.
I talk about God's wisdom,
something secret and hidden,
something God disclosed from all eternity for our glory.
    (1 Corinthians 2:6–7)

Again I heard a voice from heaven
instructing me, and it said:
Write what I tell you in this manner:
And I saw amid the fairs of the south
in the mystery of God
a beautiful, wondrous
image with a human form;
her face was so lovely and luminous
that it would be easier to look into the sun.
On her head she had
a broad circlet of gold.
And the figure spoke:
I am the great and fiery energy,

I have kindled every living spark,
and I have extinguished nothing mortal,
for I judge these things as they are.
I have determined the cosmos,
flying around the circling circles
with my upper wings,
that is, with Wisdom.
I am the fiery life of divinity,
I blaze above the beautiful fields
I shine in the water,
I burn in the sun, the moon, and the stars.

> (Hildegard of Bingen, *Book of Divine Works* 1:1; Sheryl Kujawa-Holbrook, trans., *Hildegard of Bingen: Essential Writings and Chants of a Christian Mystic—Annotated & Explained*, p. 31)

In a true vision of the spirit in a waking state:
I saw a likeness of the most beautiful girl
with her face so aglow with a splendid brightness
that I could not really look upon her.
Her cloak was whiter than snow
and brighter than a star.
She held the sun and the moon in her right hand
and she embraced them tenderly.
And I heard a voice saying to me:
The girl whom you see is Divine Love,
who abides in eternity.
For when God wished to create the world
the One bent down in tenderest love
and foresaw every need,
just like a parent preparing an inheritance for his child.
In this way the One carried out all works
in a great burning fire of love.
Thus all creatures in every species
and form acknowledge their creator,
because Love was the primal stuff

from which every creature was made.

When God said: "Let it be done," it was done,

because Divine Love was the matrix from which every creature was made,

in the blink of an eye.

> (Hildegard of Bingen, "To Abbot Adam of Ebrach, c. 1166"; *Epistolarium* [Letters] 85 R/A; Sheryl Kujawa-Holbrook, trans., *Hildegard of Bingen: Essential Writings and Chants of a Christian Mystic—Annotated & Explained*, p. 37)

And I saw three forms,

two of them standing in the clearest fountain,

encircled and crowned above by a round, porous stone.

One was in shimmering purple,

and the other was in dazzling white.

The third stood outside that fountain

and beneath the stone,

dressed in glowing white.

And the first image said:

I am Love, the light of the living God,

and Wisdom carries out her tasks along with me.

In the shadow,

Wisdom measures out all things equally,

so that one thing may not outbalance another,

and so that nothing may be moved by another into its opposite.

For Wisdom rules and constrains

every sort of diabolical malice.

In herself and through herself alone

she made all things lovingly and gently.

They can be destroyed by no enemy,

because she sees most truly

the beginning and the end of all things—

she who fully composed all things

so that all things might be ruled by her.

> (Hildegard of Bingen, *Book of Divine Works*; Sheryl Kujawa-Holbrook, trans., *Hildegard of Bingen: Essential Writings and Chants of a Christian Mystic—Annotated & Explained*, p. 53)

If your concern for others
exceeds your desire for wisdom,
your wisdom will endure.
If your desire for wisdom
exceeds your concern for others,
your wisdom will not endure.

(*Pirke Avot* 3:11; *Ethics of the Sages: Pirke Avot—Annotated & Explained*, p. 47)

If your kindness exceeds your wisdom,
your wisdom will endure.
If your wisdom exceeds your kindness,
your wisdom will not endure.

(*Pirke Avot* 3:12; *Ethics of the Sages: Pirke Avot—Annotated & Explained*, p. 47)

CHAPTER FIVE

Who Are the Wise?

Identifying the Voices of Wisdom

The wise are those who see through Einstein's optical delusion of separateness (see the previous chapter) and into the simple truth of our interbeing in, with, and as *being* itself. The wise exist in every age and in every tradition.

The Jewish tradition holds that there are always thirty-six wise human beings alive on the planet, and if not for their wisdom and the compassion that comes with it, human civilization would crumble under the weight of its collective ignorance, arrogance, and greed. The number thirty-six was chosen because in Hebrew the word *chai*, "life," carries the numerical value eighteen. The wise live not only for themselves but for others as well, hence the doubling of *chai* (eighteen) to *lamed vav* (thirty-six). These *lamed-vavniks* (thirty-sixers) understand and embody Rabbi Hillel's teaching of two thousand years ago: "If I am not for myself, who will be for me? But if I am only for myself, what am I? And if not now, when?" (*Pirke Avot* 1:14).

In Buddhism the wise are often called *bodhisattvas*, from two Sanskrit words, *sattva* (a being) of *bodhi* (enlightenment). *Bodhisattvas* devote themselves to awakening others. There are three kinds of *bodhisattvas*:

1. Those who become enlightened first in order to help others do the same
2. Those who become enlightened as they help others do the same
3. Those who become enlightened only after they have helped all others to do the same.

In all three cases the point is never one's own awakening, but that of others. As the first of the four *bodhisattva* vows puts it: *Sentient beings are innumerable. I vow to save them all.*

In Hinduism the wise are called *gurus*, "those who impart wisdom." In the Advayataraka Upanishad we are told, "The sound *gu* means 'darkness,' the sound *ru* means 'the dispeller of darkness.' Because of the power to dispel darkness and ignorance the guru is so called" (Advayataraka Upanishad, verse 16). The centrality of the guru in one's quest for knowledge is promoted in the Katha Upanishad: "When taught by one inferior in wisdom, the Self is hard to fathom. But when taught by one who is at one with Brahma [Ultimate Reality], you can be certain of realizing it" (Katha Upanishad 1.2.8).

The wise in Christianity are often associated with the Desert Mothers and Fathers, third- to sixth-century ascetics who lived primarily in the Egyptian wilderness. These early Christians took to the desert as a kind of martyrdom, abandoning material goods and physical comfort, and devoting their lives to God. As their reputation for godliness grew, thousands of people sought them out and, over time, created Christian monasticism from which others among the wise emerged.

Islam is filled with saints, sheikhs and sheikhas, not to mention the Prophet Muhammad himself (Peace Be Upon Him), who embody not only the parochial teachings of Islam but also the perennial wisdom of Allah. Indeed, one of the names of Allah is *al-Hakim*, "the Wise," and all who become wise do so through God.

In Zen the wise are called "persons of no rank"; in Taoism and Confucianism they are "the superior ones"—not superior in rank but in their capacity to see clearly.

The wise are often found among clergy, but not all clergy are wise. And they are found among laity, but not all laypeople are wise. The wise are found wherever someone is awake to what is and willing to counsel others on how to see what is for themselves.

The following texts explore what it is to be wise.

Enlightened ones are solid like the earth that endures,

steadfast like a well-set column of stone,

clear as a lake where all the mud has settled.

They are liberated from the world of life, death, and impermanence.

As a result of the freedom they have attained

through knowledge of the truth,

their thoughts are peaceful,

their words are peaceful,

and their deeds are peaceful.

> (Dhammapada 96; Max Müller, trans., revised by Jack Maguire,
> *Dhammapada: Annotated & Explained*, p. 31)

Those who are free from illusion,

who have seen the infinite void,

who have ceased to cling to impermanent things,

who have removed temptations, and who have renounced desires—

they are indeed the greatest ones of all.

> (Dhammapada 97; Max Müller, trans., revised by Jack Maguire,
> *Dhammapada: Annotated & Explained*, p. 33)

Wherever enlightened ones dwell—

in a village or wilderness,

on a mountain or on a coast—

that is indeed a place of joy.

In forests where others find no delight,

there they will know delight.

Because they do not look for pleasure,

they will have it.

> (Dhammapada 98–99; Max Müller, trans., revised by Jack Maguire,
> *Dhammapada: Annotated & Explained*, p. 33)

For you who seek the heights of spiritual meditation,
practice is the only method,
and when you have attained them,
you must remain in continual self-control.
When you renounce even the thought of initiating action,
when you are not interested in sense objects
or any results which may flow from your actions,
then in truth you understand spirituality.

> (Bhagavad Gita 6:3–4; Shri Purohit Swami, trans., *Bhagavad Gita: Annotated & Explained*, p. 49)

Seek liberation by the help of your highest Self,
and never disgrace your own Self.
For that Self is your only friend,
yet it may also be your enemy.
To you who have conquered your lower nature by its help,
the Self is a friend, but to you who had not done so, it is an enemy.

> (Bhagavad Gita 6:5–6; Shri Purohit Swami, trans., *Bhagavad Gita: Annotated & Explained*, p. 49)

The Self of one who is self-controlled
and has attained peace
is equally unmoved by heat or cold,
pleasure or pain, honor or dishonor.
[This one] desires nothing but wisdom and spiritual insight,
and looks impartially on all—lover, friend, or foe,
indifferent or hostile; alien or relative;
virtuous or sinful.

> (Bhagavad Gita 6:7–9; Shri Purohit Swami, trans., *Bhagavad Gita: Annotated & Explained*, pp. 49, 51)

You who sees Me in everything and everything in Me,
you shall I never forsake, nor shall you lose Me.

You who realizes the unity of life and
who worships Me in all beings,
lives in Me, whatever may be your lot.

> (Bhagavad Gita 6:30–32; Shri Purohit Swami, trans., *Bhagavad Gita:*
> *Annotated & Explained*, p. 49)

The wise say that the Unmanifest and Indestructible
is the highest goal of all;
when once that is reached, there is no return.
That is My Blessed Home.
That Highest God, in whom all beings abide,
and who pervades the entire universe,
is reached only by whole-hearted devotion.

> (Bhagavad Gita 8:21–22; Shri Purohit Swami, trans., *Bhagavad Gita:*
> *Annotated & Explained*, p. 69)

The one who is the conqueror and cannot be conquered,
the one whose conquest no one in this world can challenge—
by what track can you lead this person:
the awakened, the all-seeing, the trackless?
The one whom no desire with its snares and poisons can lead astray,
by what track can you lead this person:
the awakened, the all-seeing, the trackless?
Even the gods envy those who are awakened and not forgetful,
who are given to meditation, who are wise,
and who delight in the repose of retirement from the world.

> (Dhammapada 14:179–181; Max Müller, trans., revised by Jack Maguire,
> *Dhammapada: Annotated & Explained*, p. 59)

Those who possess compassion and wisdom,
who are just, speak the truth,
and take responsibility for themselves—
those the world holds dear.

Those who aspire to oneness with the absolute,
who are peaceful in their minds,
and whose thoughts are not bewildered by desires—
they are called those who are heading upstream.

> (Dhammapada 217–218; Max Müller, trans., revised by Jack Maguire,
> *Dhammapada: Annotated & Explained*, pp. 67, 69)

People cannot be called wise
because they talk a great deal.
The person who is patient
and free from hatred or fear—
that person is truly wise.

> (Dhammapada 258; Max Müller, trans., revised by Jack Maguire,
> *Dhammapada: Annotated & Explained*, p. 81)

Shimon ben Gamliel teaches,
I was raised on the talk of sages,
and yet I find nothing more true than silence.
Action, not words, is the main thing,
and excessive talk leads to error and delusion.

> (*Pirke Avot* 1:17; *Ethics of the Sages: Pirke Avot—Annotated & Explained*, p. 17)

People cannot be called elders
just because their hair is gray.
Their age may be ripe,
but they are more rightly called "old-in-vain."
The one in whom there is also
truth, goodness, gentleness, self-control, and moderation,
the one who is steadfast and free from impurity—
that one is rightly called an elder.

> (Dhammapada 259–260; Max Müller, trans., revised by Jack Maguire,
> *Dhammapada: Annotated & Explained*, p. 81)

One is not a sage
because one observes silence
if one is also foolish and ignorant;
but the one who, weighing the balance,
chooses the good and rejects the evil—
that person is a sage and for that very reason.
The one who understands both alternatives
is therefore called a sage.

> (Dhammapada 268–269; Max Müller, trans., revised by Jack Maguire,
> *Dhammapada: Annotated & Explained*, p. 83)

One is not a great one
because one defeats or harms other living beings.
One is so called because one refrains from defeating
or harming other living beings.

> (Dhammapada 270; Max Müller, trans., revised by Jack Maguire,
> *Dhammapada: Annotated & Explained*, p. 83)

Tzu-kung asked what constituted the Noble Person.
The Master said,
Noble Persons act before speaking
and afterwards speak according to their actions.

> (Analects II:13; James Legge, trans., revised by Rodney L. Taylor,
> *Confucius, the Analects: The Path of the Sage—Selections Annotated & Explained*,
> p. 23)

The Master said,
The Noble Person is
broad-minded and not prejudiced.
The petty person is
prejudiced and not broad-minded.

> (Analects II:14; James Legge, trans., revised by Rodney L. Taylor,
> *Confucius, the Analects: The Path of the Sage—Selections Annotated & Explained*,
> p. 23)

Noble Persons do not,

even for the space of a single meal,

act contrary to goodness.

In moments of haste, they cleave to it.

In seasons of danger, they cleave to it.

> (Analects IV:5; James Legge, trans., revised by Rodney L. Taylor,
> *Confucius, the Analects: The Path of the Sage—Selections Annotated & Explained*,
> p. 25)

The Master said,

Noble Persons in the world do not set themselves

either for things or against things;

they simply follow what is right.

> (Analects IV:10; James Legge, trans., revised by Rodney L. Taylor,
> *Confucius, the Analects: The Path of the Sage—Selections Annotated & Explained*,
> p. 25)

The Master said,

The Noble Person cherishes virtue;

the petty person cherishes comfort:

the Noble Person cherishes the law;

the petty person cherishes favors.

> (Analects IV:11; James Legge, trans., revised by Rodney L. Taylor,
> *Confucius, the Analects: The Path of the Sage—Selections Annotated & Explained*,
> p. 27)

The Master said,

The Noble Person is cautious in words,

but deliberate in actions.

> (Analects IV: 24; James Legge, trans., revised by Rodney L. Taylor,
> *Confucius, the Analects: The Path of the Sage—Selections Annotated & Explained*,
> p. 27)

Confucius said,
There are three things that
Noble Persons guard against.
In youth when the physical powers
are not yet settled,
they guard against lust.
When they are strong,
and the physical powers are full of vigor,
they guard against quarrelsomeness.
When they are old,
and the physical powers are decayed,
they guard against covetousness.

    (Analects XVI:7; James Legge, trans., revised by Rodney L. Taylor,
    Confucius, the Analects: The Path of the Sage—Selections Annotated & Explained,
    p. 43)

Amma Theodora said,
Power, vanity, and pride
have no place in a teacher's heart.
Immune to flattery, bribery, coercion, and fear,
they are slow to anger, calm, and self-effacing.
Relaxed and neutral,
they care for all and love every soul.

    (Theodora 5; *Apophthegmata Patrum* [Sayings of the Desert Fathers])

Amma Syncletica said,
Teachers who have not mastered their passions
are a threat to their students.
Studying with them is like attending a gala
in a house on the verge of collapse.
While their words may bring insight,
their lack of self-control can yet cause great harm.

    (Syncletica 12; *Apophthegmata Patrum* [Sayings of the Desert Fathers])

Abba Isaac said,

Though I can be hurt by others,

I never allow my thoughts to be marred with revenge.

Though I can hurt others,

I make peace with them quickly

that their thoughts too remain calm and undistracted.

> (Isaac, Priest of the Cells 9; *Apophthegmata Patrum* [Sayings of the Desert Fathers])

Abba Poemen said that Abba John said that

the saints are like a group of trees,

each bearing different fruit

but watered from the same source.

The practices of one saint differ from those of another,

but it is the same Spirit that works in all of them.

> (John the Dwarf 43; *Apophthegmata Patrum* [Sayings of the Desert Fathers])

Abba Poemen asked of Abba Joseph,

How is one to become a monk?

Abba Joseph replied,

Rest in the question, "Who am I?"

and refrain from judging anyone.

> (Joseph of Panephysis 2; *Apophthegmata Patrum* [Sayings of the Desert Fathers])

Abba Lot inquired of Abba Joseph,

What is a true monk?

Abba Joseph said,

A true monk is a raging fire.

Abba Lot replied,

I fast a bit and pray,

I contemplate and cleanse my mind of distractions.

I cultivate peace to the best of my ability.

What more can I do?
Abba Joseph stood, raised his hands skyward,
and allowed his fingers to turn to flame.
He then said,
If you choose you can become pure fire.

> (Joseph of Panephysis 6–7; *Apophthegmata Patrum* [Sayings of the Desert
> Fathers])

God has given me certain knowledge of the way things are:
to know how the world was made,
and the operation of the elements.
I know a thing's beginning, middle, and end.
I understand the alternating of sun and moon,
and the turning of seasons.
The cycle of the year is known to me,
and the positions of the constellations.
The nature of living things, the passion of wild beasts,
the violence of storms, the rationalizations of human beings,
and the healing power of roots;
all things both hidden and revealed, are known to me.

> (Wisdom of Solomon 7:17–21; *The Divine Feminine in Biblical Wisdom Literature:
> Selections Annotated & Explained*, p. 123)

Not all silence is the same.
Some are silent and thought wise,
while others are despised because they speak.
Some are silent because they don't know what to say,
while others are silent because they know when not to speak.
The wise keep quiet until the moment for speaking is ripe.
The fool babbles without regard to the time and season.
The babbler will be detested.
The self-proclaimed authority will be despised.

> (Sirach 20:5–8; *The Divine Feminine in Biblical Wisdom Literature:
> Selections Annotated & Explained*, p. 155)

At first I was like a narrow stream from a river,
and as a shallow brook into a garden.
I said, I will water my best garden,
I will moisten my finest beds.
Then my brook became a river,
and my river became a sea.
In this way I make instruction glisten in the morning,
its shimmering seen from afar.
I pour out teaching as prophecy,
and leave it for future generations.
Know this: I do not labor for myself alone,
but for all you who seek Wisdom.

> (Sirach 24:30–34; *The Divine Feminine in Biblical Wisdom Literature: Selections Annotated & Explained*, p. 149)

A true monk is one
who has achieved watchfulness;
and you who are truly watchful
are a monk in your heart.

> (Saint Hesychios the Priest I, "One Watchfulness and Holiness," sec. 159; *Philokalia*)

Judge your thoughts
to know which are wise and which are foolish.
Enshrine the wise in your soul, and treasure them.
Subject the foolish to the blade of intellect,
shatter them in prayer and meditation,
and allow them no place in your soul.
Only one who consistently examines thought
can be called a lover of the Way.

> (Saint Theodoros the Great Ascetic II, "A Century of Spiritual Texts," sec. 70; *Philokalia*)

We send the Messengers only
to give good news and to warn,
so those who believe and mend their ways
have nothing to fear,
and they will not sorrow.

> (Qur'an 6:48; Yusuf Ali, trans., revised by Sohaib N. Sultan, *The Qur'an and Sayings of the Prophet Muhammad: Selections Annotated & Explained*, p. 39)

We sent not a messenger
except to teach
in the language of the messenger's own people
in order to bring them
clarity of understanding.

> (Qur'an 14:4; Yusuf Ali, trans., revised by Sohaib N. Sultan, *The Qur'an and Sayings of the Prophet Muhammad: Selections Annotated & Explained*, p. 39)

For We assuredly sent
amongst every people a Messenger,
telling them to serve God, and abstain from evil.
Of the people were some whom God guided,
and some who inevitably went astray.
So travel through the earth
and see what the end was of those
who rejected the truth.

> (Qur'an 16:36; Yusuf Ali, trans., revised by Sohaib N. Sultan, *The Qur'an and Sayings of the Prophet Muhammad: Selections Annotated & Explained*, p. 39)

Heaven and Earth are everlasting
The reason Heaven and Earth can last forever
Is that they do not exist for themselves

Thus they can last forever
Therefore the sages:
Place themselves last but end up in front
Are outside of themselves and yet survive
Is it not all due to their selflessness?
That is how they can achieve their own goals

    (Tao Te Ching 7; Derek Lin, trans., *Tao Te Ching: Annotated & Explained*, p. 15)

Those who would be first shall be last,
and those who would be last shall be first.

    (Matthew 20:16)

Yield and remain whole
Bend and remain straight
Be low and become filled
Be worn out and become renewed
Have little and receive
Have much and be confused
Therefore the sages hold to the one as an example for the world
Without flaunting themselves—and so are seen clearly
Without presuming themselves—and so are distinguished
Without praising themselves—and so have merit
Without boasting about themselves—and so are lasting
Because they do not contend, the world cannot contend with them
What the ancients called "the one who yields and remains whole"
Were they speaking empty words?
Sincerity becoming whole, and returning to oneself

    (Tao Te Ching 22; Derek Lin, trans., *Tao Te Ching: Annotated & Explained*, p. 45)

Those who understand others are intelligent
Those who understand themselves are enlightened
Those who overcome others have strength

Those who overcome themselves are powerful
Those who know contentment are wealthy
Those who proceed vigorously have willpower
Those who do not lose their base endure
Those who die but do not perish have longevity
  (Tao Te Ching 33; Derek Lin, trans., *Tao Te Ching: Annotated & Explained*, p. 15)

Those who know do not talk
Those who talk do not know
Close the mouth
Shut the doors
Blunt the sharpness
Unravel the knots
Dim the glare
Mix the dust
This is called Mystic Oneness
They cannot obtain this and be closer
They cannot obtain this and be distant
They cannot obtain this and be benefited
They cannot obtain this and be harmed
They cannot obtain this and be valued
They cannot obtain this and be degraded
Therefore, they become honored by the world
  (Tao Te Ching 56; Derek Lin, trans., *Tao Te Ching: Annotated & Explained*,
  p. 113)

Act without action
Manage without meddling
Taste without tasting
Great, small, many, few
Respond to hatred with virtue
Plan difficult tasks through the simplest tasks
Achieve large tasks through the smallest tasks
The difficult tasks of the world

Must be handled through the simple tasks
The large tasks of the world
Must be handled through the small tasks
Therefore, sages never attempt great deeds all through life
Thus they can achieve greatness
One who makes promises lightly must deserve little trust
One who sees many easy tasks must encounter much difficulty
Therefore, sages regard things as difficult
So they never encounter difficulties all through life

> (Tao Te Ching 63; Derek Lin, trans., *Tao Te Ching: Annotated & Explained*,
> p. 127)

To know that you do not know is highest
To not know but think you know is flawed
Only when one recognizes the fault as a fault
can one be without fault
The sages are without fault
Because they recognize the fault as a fault
That is why they are without fault

> (Tao Te Ching 71; Derek Lin, trans., *Tao Te Ching: Annotated & Explained*,
> p. 143)

Shammai teaches,
Discipline yourself to study wisdom;
say little and do much;
welcome everyone with grace.

> (*Pirke Avot* 1:15; *Ethics of the Sages: Pirke Avot—Annotated & Explained*, p. 15)

Let your thoughts of boundless love pervade the whole world.

> (Nipata Sutta 150)

CHAPTER SIX

The Way

Discovering a Path to Wisdom

The Way is how the wise become wise. The Way is not a fixed set of disciplines, prescriptions, commandments, or laws. The Way is more strategy than tactic. And because it is, it is all the more difficult to master.

The Way is not a particular way—a way that can be packaged, sold, and followed as one might follow a recipe to bake a cake. Rather, the Way is your way, the way you find useful for awakening to the Truth manifesting in you, with you, and around you here and now.

Moses speaks of the Way when he says:

> Do not imagine this teaching is too difficult for you, or that it is beyond your reach. It is not in the sky that you might say, "Who is capable of flying up into the sky to secure it for us that we might hear it and live it?" Nor is it beyond the ocean that you might say, "Who can cross the sea to secure it for us that we might hear it and live it?" On the contrary! The word is very near you: in your mouth and in your heart, that you may do it. (Deuteronomy 30:11–14)

And Jesus speaks of the Way when he says:

> If your leaders say to you, "Look! The Kingdom is in the sky!" then the birds of the sky will be there before you are. If they say that the Kingdom is in the sea, then the fish will be there before you are. Rather, the Kingdom is within you and it is outside of you. (Gospel of Thomas 3)

The kingdom of God will not arrive with signs to be fathomed so that people will say, "Look! Here it is!" Or, "Look! There it is!" No, the kingdom of God is already in your midst. (Luke 17:20–21)

And the Qur'an speaks of the Way when it teaches that God is nearer to you than your jugular vein (Qur'an 50:16).

The point is that the Way *to* Truth is the Way *of* Truth; you do not arrive at the kingdom of heaven but rather live the kingdom of heaven wherever you happen to be at this and every moment: "God is with you wherever you are" (Qur'an 57:4).

Tao is obscured by partial accomplishments;
speech is obscured by flowery language.
Thus we now have the contentions of different philosophical schools—
one saying "right" where the other says "wrong," and vice versa.
To decide on what is actually right and what is in fact wrong,
it is best to shine an impartial light on things.

    (Chuang-tzu 2; Livia Kohn, trans., *Chuang-tzu: The Tao of Perfect Happiness—
    Selections Annotated & Explained*, p. 17)

The Way is not difficult
for those who have no preferences.
When love and hate are both absent,
everything becomes clear and undisguised.
Make the following distinction, however,
and heaven and earth are set infinitely apart.
If you wish to see the truth, cease to hold opinions.
To set up what you like against what you dislike
is the disease of the mind.

    (Hsin Hsin Ming, Third Chinese Patriarch of Zen)

Who is able to grasp the Way?
Only those with pure hearts
and single-purpose minds.
  (Kevaddha Sutta)

When the senses and the mind are stilled,
when the intellect rests in silence,
then the great path begins.
  (Katha Upanishad)

The One Who Is says:
Of what value is the carved image
even to the carver?
Molten statues teach you nothing,
so why do you trust in idols?
Only a fool says to wood,
"Wake up!"
or to lifeless stone,
"Arise!"
Can a coating of gold and silver
disguise the fact that there is no breath within it?
But I reside in My holy abode—
Be silent before Me all the earth!
  (Habakkuk 2:18–20; *The Hebrew Prophets: Selections Annotated & Explained*,
  p. 47)

The Ineffable says:
Invoke Me, the Ineffable One,
as All in all.
Return to Me!
Practice compassion and justice, and trust in Me always.
  (Hosea 12:7; *The Hebrew Prophets: Selections Annotated & Explained*, p. 53)

The way of God is smooth;
the wise walk effortlessly,
the foolish stumble needlessly.

    (Hosea 14:10; *The Hebrew Prophets: Selections Annotated & Explained*, p. 57)

The Ineffable says:
If you place your trust in the transient,
if you take refuge in flesh and blood rather than in Me,
you are doomed.
You will become like scrub in the desert,
having no joy,
living only in scorched and barren wilderness.
Blessed are you who trust in Me,
and in Me alone.
You are like trees rooted near water.
Your leaves are evergreen
and yield fruit in its season.
You have no fear of drought.
Who can fathom the devious perversity of the heart?
I probe the heart,
and search the mind,
and allow you to reap what you sow.

    (Jeremiah 17:5–10; *The Hebrew Prophets: Selections Annotated & Explained*,
    p. 63)

The Ineffable says:
"Come out and stand before Me."
Suddenly the Ineffable passed by.
A huge and powerful tornado swept by Elijah,
splitting mountains and shattering rocks,
but the Ineffable was not in the tornado.
The tornado passed,

followed by a violent quaking of the earth,
but the Ineffable was not in the earthquake.
The earth grew still
and a roaring fire consumed the earth;
but the Ineffable was not in the blaze.
Then the fire burned out,
replaced by a fragile silence.
Elijah heard it,
and wrapped his cloak about his face
and stood at the mouth of the cave.
Then a voice addressed him:
"Why are you here, Elijah?"

> (1 Kings 19:11–13; *The Hebrew Prophets: Selections Annotated & Explained*, p. 11)

The Ineffable says:
Do not imitate the way of fools.
Do not distract yourself with zodiacs and signs,
no matter how many are captivated by them.
You are deluded by the wisdom of fools.
Your faith is in the work of your own hands.
You cut down trees in the forest with an ax,
adorn them with silver and gold,
fasten them with nails and hammer
so as to keep them from tottering.
These are your gods!
They are like scarecrows for frightening birds.
They do not speak.
They cannot walk.
They can do no harm and intend you no good;
and yet you are afraid of them.

> (Jeremiah 10:1–5; *The Hebrew Prophets: Selections Annotated & Explained*, p. 25)

The Ineffable says:
I know the plans I have set for you:
plans for your welfare, not your destruction.
My desire is for a future filled with hope.
When you call Me,
when you follow Me,
when you pray to Me,
I will listen.
When you seek Me you will find Me,
providing that you seek Me with a whole heart.
I am available to you, and I will restore your fortunes.
I will gather you in from your places of captivity,
and I will bring you home from your places of exile,
Call Me, and I will answer you.
I will reveal to you wondrous things;
secrets that surpass your understanding.

   (Jeremiah 33:3; *The Hebrew Prophets: Selections Annotated & Explained*, p. 67)

I love those who love Me,
and reveal myself fully to those who search Me out.

   (Proverbs 8:17; *Proverbs: Annotated & Explained*, p. 53)

Ask, and it will be given to you;
seek, and you will find;
knock, and it will be opened to you.
For all who ask receive,
and all who seek find,
and to those who knock
it will be opened.

   (Matthew 7:7–8)

Abba Macarius when asked how we should pray replied,
Keep your words simple and few.
Lift your arms to God and say,
"You will all that is and know all that is—have compassion!"
And if this is not sufficient to quiet your soul
simply cry out to God, "Help me!"
God knows what you need,
and God's mercy will see that you receive it.

    (Macarius 19; *Apophthegmata Patrum* [Sayings of the Desert Fathers])

The Ineffable One says:
Even before you pray,
I will answer;
even as you ask,
I will respond.

    (Isaiah 65:24; *The Hebrew Prophets: Selections Annotated & Explained*, p. 161)

God knows what you need
even before you ask.

    (Matthew 6:8)

And if My servants ask you about Me—
witness, I am near;
I respond to the call of those who call,
whenever they call Me:
let them, then, respond to Me,
and have faith in Me,
so that they may follow the right way.

    (Qur'an 2:186; Camille Helminski, trans., *The Light of Dawn: Daily Readings from the Holy Qur'an*, p. 26)

The prophet Micah says:
With what shall you approach the Ineffable?
How shall you humble yourself
before the Transcendent One?
Shall you seek to appease God
with burnt offerings, with yearling calves?
Would the Ineffable be appeased
with thousands of rams,
with tens of thousands of streams of oil?
Shall you give over your firstborn
to atone for your transgression,
the fruit of your belly for the error of your heart?
God has told you what is good.
What does the Ineffable require of you?
Only that you do justly
and love kindness,
and walk humbly with your [understanding of] God.

    (Micah 6:6–9; *The Hebrew Prophets: Selections Annotated & Explained*, p. 73)

Jesus said:
Seekers should not stop until they find.
When they find, they will be disturbed.
After having been disturbed, they will be astonished.
Then they will reign over everything.

    (Gospel of Thomas 2; Stevan Davies, trans., *The Gospel of Thomas: Annotated & Explained*, p. 3)

Jesus said:
Come to me,
You who are tired and burdened,
and I will give you rest.
Yoke yourself to me and learn from me,
for I am gentle and humble in heart,

and you will find rest for your souls.
My yoke is easy,
my burden is light.
    (Matthew 11:28–30)

If you have a little knowledge
Walking on the great Tao
You fear only to deviate from it
The great Tao is broad and plain
But people like the side paths
    (Tao Te Ching 53; Derek Lin, trans., *Tao Te Ching: Annotated & Explained*,
      p. 107)

My words are easy to understand, easy to practice
The world cannot understand, cannot practice
    (Tao Te Ching 70; Derek Lin, trans., *Tao Te Ching: Annotated & Explained*,
      p. 141)

O Humanity,
so long as you call upon Me and ask of Me,
I shall forgive you for what you have done,
and I shall not mind.
O Humanity,
were your sins to reach the clouds of the sky
and were you then to ask forgiveness of Me,
I would forgive you.
O Humanity,
were you to come to Me with sins
nearly as great as the earth,
and were you then to face Me,
I would bring you forgiveness nearly as great.
    (Hadith; Yusuf Ali, trans., revised by Sohaib N. Sultan, *The Qur'an and
      Sayings of the Prophet Muhammad: Selections Annotated & Explained*, p. 15)

Don't conform yourself to this present world
but transform your consciousness
so that you will be aligned with God's will,
knowing what is good,
what is acceptable to God,
and what is fully evolved.

> (Romans 12:2; Ron Miller, trans., *The Sacred Writings of Paul:*
> *Annotated & Explained*, p. 47)

If you find encouragement in the Messiah,
if you find loving comfort,
if you find spiritual fellowship,
if you find altruistic compassion,
then fill up my cup of joy by being of one mind,
sharing one love,
living as fellow souls with a common understanding.
Don't compete or boast.
Be truly humble
and see others as better than yourselves.
I don't want to see each of you looking out
only for your own interests;
rather be concerned about the interests of others.

> (Philippians 2:1–4; Ron Miller, trans., *The Sacred Writings of Paul:*
> *Annotated & Explained*, p. 49)

I encourage you, my good friends,
To fill your minds with whatever is true,
God-centered, holy, beautiful, and worthwhile.
Think about all those things that are
virtuous and praiseworthy.
In this way the God of peace will be with you.

> (Philippians 4:8–9; Ron Miller, trans., *The Sacred Writings of Paul:*
> *Annotated & Explained*, p. 51)

I have three treasures
I hold on to them and protect them
The first is called compassion
The second is called conservation
The third is called not daring to be ahead in the world

(Tao Te Ching 67; Derek Lin, trans., *Tao Te Ching: Annotated & Explained*,
p. 135)

Protect you heart from evil,
and defend your senses from defilement.
Take refuge in the peace of God
resting at the core of your being.
Monitor your thoughts,
and root out those that dull your intellect,
leaving you vulnerable to foolishness.
Only then can you remain strong in prayer,
and calm in the face of evil.

(Saint Isaiah the Solitary I, "On Guarding the Intellect," sec. 12; *Philokalia*)

The sign of true devotion is the end of conceit
and the illusion that you are already aligned with God's will.
The sign of true devotion is a rebuking conscience
forever pointing out where you are acting contrary to holiness.
In time, if your devotion is true,
your prayer will be free from rebuke,
and you will enter the peace of God.

(Saint Isaiah the Solitary I, "On Guarding the Intellect," sec. 18; *Philokalia*)

Your heart fills with thoughts
couched in images reflecting the world of the senses.

Enlightenment requires an empty heart free from form:
a clear mind cleansed of all abstraction.

> (Hesychios the Priest I, "On Watchfulness and Holiness," sec. 89;
> *Philokalia*)

The ultimate refuge is a heart undisturbed by distractions,
empowerd by Spirit, and rooted in holiness.
While few of us may find such refuge in this life,
it is awaiting us in the next.
While few of us can be a sanctuary in and of ourselves,
we can be a stone in a supporting wall.

> (Saint Gregory of Sinai IV, "On Commandment and Doctrines," sec. 7;
> *Philokalia*)

The harassment of distracting passions
is beyond your control,
and hence there is no sin in experiencing them.
Sin arises when you are weak and ineffective,
and fail to root out rebellious thoughts
before they kindle the fires of rebellious action.

> (Saint Theodoros the Great Ascetic II, "A Century of Spiritual Texts,"
> sec 9; *Philokalia*)

If you would quiet your heart
assess it with the same equanimity
you use when looking at your image in a mirror:
see the good and the bad,
and know that both are you.

> (Hesychios the Priest I, "On Watchfulness and Holiness," sec. 48;
> *Philokalia*)

You need four horses to pull the chariot of self to heaven:
peace, devotion, compassion, and restraint.

> (Saint Thalassios the Libyan II, "On Love, Self-Control, and Life in
> Accordance with the Intellect," sec. 24; *Philokalia*)

You need four tools to uproot the distracting passions:
self-restraint, love of others, forbearance, and equanimity.

> (Saint Thalassios the Libyan II, "On Love, Self-Control, and Life in
> Accordance with the Intellect," sec. 8; *Philokalia*)

Let us leave aside anger,
let us forsake pride,
let us overcome all bondage!
No sufferings befall those
who are not attached to name and form,
and who call nothing their own.
The one who holds back rising anger like a rolling chariot—
that one I call a real driver.
Other people are but holding the reins.
Let us overcome anger by love,
let us overcome evil by good,
let us overcome the greedy by generosity,
the liar by truth!
Speak the truth;
do not yield to anger;
give if you are asked,
even if you give but a little.
By these three steps you will come near the gods.

> (Dhammapada 221–224; Max Müller, trans., revised by Jack Maguire,
> *Dhammapada: Annotated & Explained*, p. 71)

If you wish to cultivate goodness and defeat evil
take stock of your actions throughout the day,

and use your evenings to make amends.

Take care to conform your deeds to godliness

and in this way not be enticed to evil

> (Saint Hesychios the Priest I, "On Watchfulness and Holiness," sec. 124;
> *Philokalia*)

The highest goodness resembles water

Water greatly benefits myriad things without contention

It stays in places that people dislike

Therefore it is similar to the Tao

Dwelling at the right place

Heart with great depth

Giving with great kindness

Words with great integrity

Governing with great administration

Handling with great capability

Moving with great timing

Because it does not contend

It is therefore beyond reproach

> (Tao Te Ching 8; Derek Lin, trans., *Tao Te Ching: Annotated & Explained*, p. 17)

Attain the ultimate emptiness

Hold on to the truest tranquility

The myriad things are all active

I therefore watch their return

Everything flourishes; each returns to its root

Returning to the root is called tranquility

Tranquility is called returning to one's nature

Returning to one's nature is called constancy

Knowing constancy is called clarity

Not knowing constancy, one recklessly causes trouble

Knowing constancy is acceptance

Acceptance is impartiality

Impartiality is sovereign

Sovereign is Heaven
Heaven is Tao
Tao is eternal
The self is no more, without danger
  (Tao Te Ching 16; Derek Lin, trans., *Tao Te Ching: Annotated & Explained*,
  p. 33)

Know the masculine, hold to the feminine
Be the watercourse of the world
Being the watercourse of the world
The eternal virtue does not depart
Return to the state of the infant
Know the white, hold to the black
Be the standard of the world
Being the standard of the world
The eternal virtue does not deviate
Return to the state of the boundless
Know the honor, hold to the humility
Be the valley of the world
Being the valley of the world
The eternal virtue shall be sufficient
Return to the state of plain wood
Plain wood splits, then becomes tools
The sages utilize them
And then become leaders
Thus the greater whole is undivided
  (Tao Te Ching 28; Derek Lin, trans., *Tao Te Ching: Annotated & Explained*,
  p. 57)

Nothing in the world is
softer or weaker than water
Yet nothing is better at
overcoming the hard and strong
[This truth is constant:]

The weak overcomes the strong
The soft overcomes the hard
Everyone knows this
But few practice it

> (Tao Te Ching Chapter 78; Derek Lin, trans., *Tao Te Ching: Annotated &*
> *Explained*, p. 157)

We need to have three kinds of knowledge:
knowledge of God;
knowledge of self;
and knowledge of where we are susceptible to fault and flaw.

> (Julian of Norwich, *Revelations of Divine Love*, 72)

While your innermost self
can deepen your knowledge of self in this world,
and while you can cultivate this knowledge
through acts of mercy and grace,
you cannot know yourself completely
until this world yields to the next.
Thus it is only wise to pray that the moment of ending,
the moment of complete knowing,
will be one of endless joy.

> (Julian of Norwich, *Revelations of Divine Love*, 46)

Knowledge of God is easier to grasp
than knowledge of your own soul.
This is because your soul is so deeply buried in God
that you cannot know the soul without first knowing God
in whom it is hidden.
If you would know your soul fully,
seek it where it may be found—in God.

> (Julian of Norwich, *Revelations of Divine Love*, 56)

If you would attain true spirituality
try unceasingly to concentrate your mind.
Make time to live in seclusion,
absolutely alone,
with mind and personality controlled,
free from desire and without possessions.

(Bhagavad Gita 6:10; Shri Purohit Swami, trans., *Bhagavad Gita: Annotated & Explained*, p. 51)

Having chosen a holy place,
sit in a firm posture on a seat
neither too high nor too low,
and covered with a grass mat, a deer skin, and a cloth.
Seated thus, your mind unwavering,
its functions controlled,
and your senses governed,
practice meditation for the purification of your lower nature.
Hold your body, head, and neck erect, motionless, and steady;
look fixedly at the tip of your nose,
turning neither to the right nor to the left.

(Bhagavad Gita 6:11–13; Shri Purohit Swami, trans., *Bhagavad Gita: Annotated & Explained*, p. 51)

Listen carefully to me, my child;
incline your ear to my teaching.
Train your eyes to see Wisdom,
and your heart to shelter Her.
These teachings give life to those who find them
and are a balm to the body of those who embrace them.
Protect your heart above all else,
for the heart determines the quality of your life.
Free yourself from hateful speech;

put aside all duplicitous talk.
Rest your eyes on the horizon,
and let your vision focus on what is next.
Keep your feet on the upright path.
Do not waver to the right or to the left;
and turn your foot away from the path of evil.

> (Proverbs 4:20–27; *Proverbs: Annotated & Explained*, p. 29)

With your heart at peace and hence fearless,
focus on Me and lose your self in Me.
Keeping your mind always in communion with Me,
and with your thoughts subdued,
you shall attain that Peace which is Mine
and which will lead you to liberation at last.

> (Bhagavad Gita 6:14–15; Shri Purohit Swami, trans., *Bhagavad Gita: Annotated & Explained*, p. 51)

When the whole of reality is seen in the light of the Self,
and you abide within your Self and are satisfied,
the mind finds rest,
and you enjoy a bliss that surpasses all understanding,
and you will never again be distracted from reality.

> (Bhagavad Gita 6:20–21; Shri Purohit Swami, trans., *Bhagavad Gita: Annotated & Explained*, p. 53)

Little by little,
by the help of your reason controlled by fortitude,
you will attain peace;
and, fixing your mind on the Self,
think of no other thing.
And if the volatile and wavering mind should wander
bring it again to its allegiance to the Self.

> (Bhagavad Gita 6:25–26; Shri Purohit Swami, trans., *Bhagavad Gita: Annotated & Explained*, p. 53)

In this way, free from sin,
abiding always in the Eternal,
you enjoy the effortless bliss
that flows from realization of the Infinite.
You will see your own Self in all beings
and all beings in your own Self,
and look upon all life with an impartial eye.
You will see Me in everything and everything in Me,
I shall never forsake you, nor shall you ever lose Me.

> (Bhagavad Gita 6:28–30; Shri Purohit Swami, trans., *Bhagavad Gita: Annotated & Explained*, pp. 53, 55)

Whatever someone offers to Me,
whether it be a leaf, or a flower, or fruit, or water,
I accept it,
for it is offered with devotion and purity of mind.
Whatever you do,
whatever you eat,
whatever you sacrifice and give,
whatever austerities you practice,
do all as an offering to Me.

> (Bhagavad Gita 9:26–27; Shri Purohit Swami, trans., *Bhagavad Gita: Annotated & Explained*, p. 75)

In whatever you eat or drink,
or in whatever else you do,
always act for God's glory.

> (1 Corinthians 10:31; Ron Miller, trans., *The Sacred Writings of Paul: Annotated & Explained*, p. 77)

Do this in remembrance of me.
  (Luke 22:19)

God guides to God
all who turn to God—
those who have faith
and whose hearts find satisfaction in the remembrance of God—
for, truly, in the remembrance of God hearts find rest.
  (Qur'an 13:28; Camille Helminski, trans., *The Light of Dawn:
  Daily Readings from the Holy Qur'an*, p. 52)

I am the same to all beings.
I favor none, and I hate none.
But those who worship Me devotedly,
they live in Me, and I in them.
Even the most sinful,
if they worship Me with a whole heart,
shall be considered righteous,
for they are treading the right path.
In time they shall attain spirituality,
and Eternal Peace shall be theirs.
  (Bhagavad Gita 9:29–31: Shri Purohit Swami, trans., *Bhagavad Gita:
  Annotated & Explained*, pp. 75, 77)

"O our Sustainer!
Do not take us to task if we forget or unknowingly do wrong!
O our Sustainer! Do not lay upon us a burden
like that which You placed on those who lived before us!
O our Sustainer! Do not make us bear burdens
which we have no strength to bear!
And efface our sins, and grant us forgiveness,
and bestow Your mercy on us!

You are our Supreme Lord:

help us when we face those who stand against truth."

> (Qur'an 2:285–6; Camille Helminski, trans., *The Light of Dawn:*
> *Daily Readings from the Holy Qur'an*, p. 7)

Fix your mind on Me,

devote yourself to Me,

sacrifice for Me,

surrender to Me,

make Me the object of your aspirations,

and you shall assuredly become one with Me,

I who am your own Self.

> (Bhagavad Gita 9:34; Shri Purohit Swami, trans., *Bhagavad Gita:*
> *Annotated & Explained*, p. 77)

Those who keep their minds fixed on Me,

who worship Me always with unwavering faith and concentration—

these are the very best.

Those who worship Me as the Indestructible,

the Undefinable, the Unmanifest, the Omnipresent,

the Unthinkable, the Primeval, the Immutable, and the Eternal;

subduing their senses,

viewing all conditions of life with the same eye,

and working for the welfare of all beings,

assuredly they come to Me.

Verily, those who surrender their actions to Me,

who muse on Me, worship Me, and meditate on Me alone,

with no thought save of Me,

I rescue them quickly from the ocean of life and death,

for their minds are fixed on Me.

Then let your mind cling only to Me,

let your intellect abide in Me;

and without doubt you shall live hereafter in Me alone.

> (Bhagavad Gita 12:2–8; Shri Purohit Swami, trans., *Bhagavad Gita:*
> *Annotated & Explained*, p. 99)

But if you cannot fix your mind firmly on Me, My beloved friend,
try to do so by constant practice.
And if you are not strong enough to practice concentration,
then devote yourself to My service,
do all your acts for My sake,
and you shall still attain the goal.
And if you are too weak even for this,
then seek refuge in union with Me,
and with perfect self-control renounce the fruit of all your action.

> (Bhagavad Gita 12:9–12; Shri Purohit Swami, trans., *Bhagavad Gita:
> Annotated & Explained*, p. 101)

If you are incapable of hatred toward any being,
if you are kind and compassionate,
free from selfishness, without pride,
equable in pleasure and in pain,
and forgiving, always contented, centered, self-controlled,
resolute, with mind and reason dedicated to Me,
you are My beloved.

> (Bhagavad Gita 12:13–14; Shri Purohit Swami, trans., *Bhagavad Gita:
> Annotated & Explained*, p. 101)

If you do no harm to the world,
and cannot be harmed by the world,
if you are not carried away
by any impulse of joy, anger, or fear,
you are My beloved.
If you are beyond joy and hate,
neither regretting nor desiring,
and accepting with equanimity the good as well as the bad,
you are My beloved.
If you treat friend and foe alike,
and welcome equally honor and dishonor,

heat and cold, pleasure and pain,

and if you are enamored of nothing,

indifferent to praise and censure,

if you enjoy silence, are contented with every fate,

and have no fixed abode,

if you are steadfast in mind

and filled with devotion,

you are My beloved.

Verily if you love the spiritual wisdom as I have taught,

if your faith never fails,

and if you concentrate your whole nature on Me,

you indeed are My most beloved.

> (Bhagavad Gita 12:13–20; Shri Purohit Swami, trans., *Bhagavad Gita: Annotated & Explained*, pp. 101, 103)

Those who submit their whole selves to God,

are beautifully excellent devotees.

They have grasped indeed the most trustworthy handhold.

And with God rests the end and decision of every affair.

> (Qur'an 31:22; Yusuf Ali, trans., revised by Sohaib N. Sultan, *The Qur'an and Sayings of the Prophet Muhammad: Selections Annotated & Explained*, p. 57)

It is good to tame the mind,

which is flighty and difficult to restrain,

rushing wherever it will.

A tamed mind brings happiness.

Let wise ones monitor the mind,

which is subtle, difficult to perceive, and restless.

A mind well monitored brings happiness.

Those who bridle their mind, which,

being insubstantial, would travel far on its own,

hidden away in the body,

are free from the bonds of evil.

> (Dhammapada 3:35–37; Max Müller, trans., revised by Jack Maguire, *Dhammapada: Annotated & Explained*, p. 13)

If your mind is free from lust and unperplexed,

if you have renounced the notions of merit and demerit,

if you remain awake and watchful,

then you never have to fear.

> (Dhammapada 3:39; Max Müller, trans., revised by Jack Maguire,
> *Dhammapada: Annotated & Explained*, p. 13)

O God!

Grant me Light in my heart,

Light in my grave,

Light in front of me,

Light behind me,

Light to my right,

Light to my left,

Light above me,

Light below me,

Light in my ears,

Light in my eyes,

Light in my skin,

Light in my hair,

Light within my flesh,

Light in my blood,

Light in my bones.

O God!

Increase my Light everywhere.

O God!

Grant me Light in my heart,

Light on my tongue,

Light in my eyes,

Light in my ears,

Light to my right,

Light to my left,

Light above me,

Light below me,

Light in front of me,
Light behind me,
And Light within my self;
Increase my Light.

> (Muhammad's Prayer of Light; Camille Helminski, trans., *The Light of Dawn: Daily Readings from the Holy Qur'an*, p. xv)

In the Name of God,
the Infinitely Compassionate,
Most Merciful.
All praise is God's,
the Sustainer of all worlds,
the Infinitely Compassionate and Most Merciful,
Sovereign of the Day of Reckoning.
You alone do we worship
and You alone do we ask for help.
Guide us on the straight path;
the path of those who have received Your favor,
not the path of those who have earned Your wrath,
nor of those who have gone astray.

> (Qur'an 1:1–7; Camille Helminski, trans., *The Light of Dawn: Daily Readings from the Holy Qur'an*, p. 1)

O Humankind!
Worship your Sustainer,
who has created you and those who lived before you,
so that you might remain conscious of the One
who has made the earth a resting place for you
and the sky a canopy,
and has sent water down from the sky
and with it brought forth fruits for your sustenance:
then don't claim that there is any power that could rival God,
when you grasp the truth.

> (Qur'an 2:21–22; Camille Helminski, trans., *The Light of Dawn: Daily Readings from the Holy Qur'an*, p. 2)

Truly: all who surrender
their whole being to God,
and do good,
shall have their reward with their Sustainer;
these need have no fear,
neither shall they grieve.

   (Qur'an 2:112; Camille Helminski, trans., *The Light of Dawn:*
   Daily Readings from the Holy Qur'an, p. 2)

O you who have attained to faith!
Seek help through steadfast patience and prayer,
for observe:
God is with those who patiently persevere.

   (Qur'an 2:153; Camille Helminski, trans., *The Light of Dawn:*
   Daily Readings from the Holy Qur'an, p. 3)

Such is God, your Sustainer:
there is no god but God,
the Creator of everything:
then worship God alone—
for it is God who has everything in God's care.
No vision can encompass God,
but God encompasses all human vision:
for God alone is
Subtle Beyond Comprehension, All-Aware.
Means of insight have now come to you
from your Sustainer through this divine Message.
Those, then, who choose to see,
do so for the benefit of their own souls;
and those who choose to remain blind,
do so to their own harm.

   (Qur'an 6:102–104; Camille Helminski, trans., *The Light of Dawn:*
   Daily Readings from the Holy Qur'an, p. 28)

Invoke God,
or invoke the Most Gracious:
by whichever name you invoke God,
God is all the attributes of perfection.
And do not be too loud in your prayer
nor speak it in too low a voice,
but follow a middle way.

> (Qur'an 17:110; Camille Helminski, trans., *The Light of Dawn:
> Daily Readings from the Holy Qur'an*, p. 69)

When asked for advice by a novice
Abba Moses said,
Take refuge in your cell.
Your cell will teach you all you need to know.

> (Moses 6; *Apophthegmata Patrum* [Sayings of the Desert Fathers])

A novice sought out Abba Hierax
and asked how he might find salvation.
Abba Hierax said,
Take refuge in your cell.
Eat if hungry. Drink if thirsty.
And speak kindly regarding everyone.
That is salvation.

> (Hierax 1; *Apophthegmata Patrum* [Sayings of the Desert Fathers])

When hungry—eat.
When tired—sleep.
This is Zen.

> (Hiakajo Roshi)

Whenever you pray
take refuge in your room and close the door.
Pray to God in secret.
And God who sees in secret will reward you.
  (Matthew 6:5–6)

When asked to explain the verse,
"I was on watch and God came to me,"
Abba John said,
Take refuge in your cell and rest your mind on God.
  (John the Dwarf 27 on Matthew 25:36; *Apophthegmata Patrum* [Sayings of
  the Desert Fathers])

Without going out the door, know the world
Without peering out the window, see the Heavenly Tao
The further one goes
The less one knows
Therefore the sage
Knows without going
Names without seeing
Achieves without striving
  (Tao Te Ching 47; Derek Lin, trans., *Tao Te Ching: Annotated & Explained*,
  p. 95)

Amma Syncletica said,
Do not imagine it is enough to withdraw into the wilderness.
There are mountain hermits
who are no less distracted than city dwellers.
And there are city dwellers
who can achieve solitude in their minds.
And while a hermit may avoid the crowds without,
the crowds within are no less distracting.
  (Syncletica 19; *Apophthegmata Patrum* [Sayings of the Desert Fathers])

Abba Moses of Skete said,
Keep your gaze on God alone.
Even a slight distraction of the heart must be corrected.

(John Cassian, *Institutes and Conferences*, 1, p. xiii)

Abba Poemen says,
A still mouth may hide a babbling mind
filled with judgment and condemnation.
A ceaseless tongue may reflect a great stillness
if what is said is nothing but truth.

(Poemen 27; *Apophthegmata Patrum* [Sayings of the Desert Fathers])

Focused prayer is the mind's straight road to God.
To cultivate this prayer abandon all distractions,
and ask to be cleansed of all passions,
freed from all foolishness,
and liberated from all seduction.

(Evagrios the Solitary I, "On Prayer," sec. 35–38; *Philokalia*)

Outer prayer—
prayer reliant upon form and gesture—
is empty.
Inner prayer—
the prayer of the heart bathed in devotion and wonder—
is the prayer that awakens the intellect to the spirit.

(Evagrios the Solitary I, "On Prayer," sec. 28; *Philokalia*)

Blessed is the mind
whose prayer is unbound by form.
Blessed is the mind

focused solely on yearning for God.

Blessed is the mind

whose prayer is not tied to things.

Blessed in the mind

whose prayer transcends the physical.

    (Evagrios the Solitary I, "On Prayer," sec. 117–120; *Philokalia*)

There are two levels of prayer prized over all others,

and the first is higher than the second.

The first is found among the contemplatives,

the second among the virtuous.

The first is generated by the soul's awe of God,

the second by the soul's longing for God.

The first cultivates a mind

that sees both self and other and yet reveals only God.

The second cultivates a mind

that sees neither self nor other, but only God.

The first sees God directly.

The second sees God's reflection.

    (Saint Maximos the Confessor II, "Second Century on Love," sec. 6;
    Philokalia)

One whose mind sees through the world of physicality

is free from form and sensation.

This one is one who prays without ceasing.

    (Saint Maximos the Confessor II, "Second Century on Love," sec. 61;
    Philokalia)

Do not imagine prayer is limited to time and space.

If you imagine prayer is done

"here" and not "there,"

  or "then" and not "now,"

your efforts "there" and "then"

will be wasted and distracting.

Prayer is cultivating a mind at one with God,

totally immersed in God.

As Saint Paul said,

Prayer unites the mind with God

until it becomes one with God (1 Corinthians 6:17).

> (Nikitas Stithatos IV, "On the Inner Nature of Things and on the
> Purification of the Intellect," sec. 77; *Philokalia*)

Stillness is a mind unperturbed by thoughts and feelings,

a spirit serene in unbounded joy,

a heart rooted deeply in God.

Rest your meditation in divine radiance.

Root your knowledge in the divine mystery.

Center your wisdom in a clear mind,

a boundless field of divine knowing.

The ecstasy of a mind at one with God

maintains awareness of God even in sleep.

True prayer brings peaceful sleep

even in times of trouble.

True prayer in the end

is an unshakable oneness with God.

> (Nikitas Stithatos IV, "On the Inner Nature of Things and on the
> Purification of the Intellect," sec. 64; *Philokalia*)

Stillness has three qualities:

restraint, silence, and humility.

Guard these carefully,

and take care never to lose them through inattention.

Each is interdependent with the other

and none can stand alone.

It is from these qualities that true prayer is born

and through them that it blossoms.

> (Saint Gregory of Sinai IV, "On Prayer," sec. 7; *Philokalia*)

Jesus said: If your leaders say to you,
"Look! The Kingdom is in the sky!"
then the birds will be there before you are.
If they say that the Kingdom is in the sea,
then the fish will be there before you are.
Rather, the Kingdom is within you and it is outside of you.

>   (Gospel of Thomas 3a; Stevan Davies, trans., *The Gospel of Thomas:*
>   *Annotated & Explained*, p. 5)

Do not imagine this teaching is too difficult for you,
or that it is beyond your reach.
It is not in the sky that you might say,
Who can fly up into the sky to secure it for us that
we might hear it and live it?
Nor is it beyond the ocean that you might say,
Who can cross the sea to secure it for us that
we might hear it and live it?
On the contrary!
The word is very near you:
in your mouth and in your heart,
that you may do it.

>   (Deuteronomy 30:11–14)

Jesus said:
I will give you that which eyes have not seen,
ears have not heard,
hands did not touch,
and minds have not conceived.

>   (Gospel of Thomas 17; Stevan Davies, trans., *The Gospel of Thomas:*
>   *Annotated & Explained*, p. 23)

Jesus saw infants being suckled.
He said to his disciples:
These infants taking milk are like
those who enter the Kingdom. His disciples asked him:
If we are infants, will we enter the Kingdom?
Jesus responded:
When you make the two into one,
and when you make the inside like the outside
and the outside like the inside,
and the upper like the lower,
and thus make the male and the female the same,
so that the male isn't male
and the female isn't female.
When you make an eye to replace an eye,
and a hand to replace a hand,
and a foot to replace a foot,
and an image to replace an image,
then you will enter the Kingdom.

> (Gospel of Thomas 22a–b; Stevan Davies, trans., *The Gospel of Thomas: Annotated & Explained*, p. 33)

His disciples asked him:
When will you appear to us?
When will we see you?
Jesus replied:
When you strip naked without shame
and trample your clothing underfoot
just as little children do,
then you will look at the child of the living One
without being afraid.

> (Gospel of Thomas 37; Stevan Davies, trans., *The Gospel of Thomas: Annotated & Explained*, p. 49)

Jesus said:

The Kingdom of the Father is

like a woman who took a little leaven

and concealed it in dough.

She made large loaves of bread.

You who have ears—hear!

> (Gospel of Thomas 96; Stevan Davies, trans., *The Gospel of Thomas: Annotated & Explained*, p. 117)

Jesus said:

When you make the two into one,

you will become fully awake.

Then when you say,

"Move, mountain!"

it will move.

> (Gospel of Thomas 106; Stevan Davies, trans., *The Gospel of Thomas: Annotated & Explained*, p. 129)

Jesus said:

All who drink from my mouth

will become as I am,

and I will become them.

And the hidden things will be revealed to them.

> (Gospel of Thomas 108; Stevan Davies, trans., *The Gospel of Thomas: Annotated & Explained*, p. 131)

His disciples asked him:

When is the Kingdom coming?

He replied:

It is not coming in an easily observable manner.

People will not be saying,

"Look, it's over here"

or "Look, it's over there."

Rather, the Kingdom is already spread out on the earth,
and people aren't aware of it.

(Gospel of Thomas 113; Stevan Davies, trans., *The Gospel of Thomas:
Annotated & Explained*, p. 137)

It is the Wisdom of God
that brings you close to the kingdom of heaven.
It is lack of repentance that distances you from it.
Cultivate the qualities of repentance:
humility and sadness over your failings,
a kind and loving heart
that follows the way of justice and goodness.
The kingdom of heaven—
or more accurately the Infinite and Unknowable sovereign of
    heaven—
is within you,
and it is to this alone that you should cling
through acts of contrition, patience,
and loving as fully as you can
the One who loves you completely.

(St. Gregory Palamas IV, "Topics of Natural and Theological Science,"
sec. 57; *Philokalia*)

While alive, the body is soft and pliant
When dead, it is hard and rigid
All living things, grass and trees,
While alive, are soft and supple
When dead, become dry and brittle
Thus that which is hard and stiff is the follower of death
That which is soft and yielding
is the follower of life
Therefore, an inflexible army will not win
A strong tree will be cut down

The big and forceful occupy a lowly position
While the soft and pliant occupy a higher place
> (Tao Te Ching 76; Derek Lin, trans., *Tao Te Ching: Annotated & Explained*,
> p. 153)

Hillel teaches,
Discipline yourself in the way of Aaron,
loving peace and pursing peace;
loving people and bringing them to Truth.
> (*Pirke Avot* 1:12; *Ethics of the Sages: Pirke Avot, Annotated & Explained*, p. 13)

Always focus your mind on the simple truth:
God dwells within you.
> (Babylonian Talmud, *Taanit* 11b)

Let your charity be done in secret.
> (Matthew 6:4)

One who gives charity in secret is greater than Moses.
> (Rabbi Eleazar, Babylonian Talmud, *Bava Batra* 9b)

Let your "Yes" mean "Yes."
Let your "No" mean "No."
> (Matthew 5:37)

Let your "Yes" be honest,
And let your "No" be honest.
> (Rabbi Jose ben Judah, Babylonian Talmud, *Bava Metzia* 49a)

CHAPTER SEVEN

Living Wisely

Dwelling in Wisdom from Day to Day

In the previous chapter we laid out the Way as strategy. In this chapter we focus on tactic: practical things you can do to live the Way and become wise. The teachings presented in the following pages are doable, even without first realizing the true nature of Ultimate Reality as God, Tao, Brahma, Allah, Self, and the Eternal I. While living the Way may awaken you to the Ultimate Reality that is your truest Self, awakening itself is not a prerequisite for living the Way.

If we were to highlight a single benchmark for living wisely it would be the Golden Rule in both its negative and positive forms: *What is hateful to you, do not do to others*; and, *do to others only what you would want others to do to you*. While a version of the Golden Rule appears in almost every religion, the Rule itself transcends religion. This becomes clear when we realize that the Golden Rule itself allows for no exceptions, yet the religions that affirm the Rule are steeped in them—especially in their treatment of women and those considered nonbelievers, heretics, or infidels.

For example, in many religions women are treated as second-class citizens, often forced to endure treatment that, if done to men, would be considered anathema. Clearly doing to women what you would want done to men is not a version of the Rule most religions support. Similarly, many forms of religion imagine an afterlife where nonbelievers, heretics, and infidels suffer eternal torture in the pits of hell, yet no member of these religions would wish to be so tortured. While the Golden Rule would outlaw such torture, many religions—even those that celebrate the Golden Rule—endorse it.

In the context of perennial wisdom, however, the Golden Rule is absolute. Any god that commands torture in this life or the next is not God. Any faith that sanctions torture in this life or the next is not wise. Any religion that promotes misogyny, homophobia, racism, xenophobia, anti-Semitism, and the like are not what the historian Karen Armstrong calls "skillful."

> The test is simple: if people's beliefs—secular or religious—make them belligerent, intolerant, and unkind about other people's faith, they are not "skillful." If, however, their convictions impel them to act compassionately and to honor the stranger, then they are good, helpful, and sound. This is the test of true religiosity in every single one of the major traditions.[1]

Albert Einstein's "true religion," which sees through the optical delusion of *us against them* into the greater truth of *us and them* and *all of us together*, and Karen Armstrong's "true religiosity," which condones nothing that is not "good, helpful, and sound," are the hallmarks of perennial wisdom and the key to the global spirituality promoted by *The World Wisdom Bible*. While every religion contains elements of the true and the sound, no religion in its entirety reflects it. Religion reflects both the wisdom and the folly to which we humans are heir. Living wisely helps you distinguish between the two and shape your life with the former even as you continually cleanse your thinking of the latter.

> All that you are
> is the result of what you have thought.
> It is founded on your thoughts.
> It is made up of your thoughts.
> If you speak or act with an evil thought,
> pain follows you,
> as the wheel follows the foot of the ox
> that draws the wagon.
>
> (Dhammapada 1; Max Müller, trans., revised by Jack Maguire,
> *Dhammapada: Annotated & Explained*, p. 3)

All that you are
is the result of what you have thought.
It is founded on your thoughts.
It is made up of your thoughts.
If you speak or act with a pure thought,
happiness follows you,
like a shadow that never leaves.

> (Dhammapada 2; Max Müller, trans., revised by Jack Maguire,
> *Dhammapada: Annotated & Explained*, p. 3)

"She abused me, he beat me,
she defeated me, he robbed me":
In those who harbor such thoughts,
hatred will never cease.
"She abused me, he beat me,
she defeated me, he robbed me":
In those who do not harbor such thoughts,
hatred will cease.
For never does hatred cease by hatred at any time.
Hatred ceases by love.
This is an eternal law.

> (Dhammapada 3–5; Max Müller, trans., revised by Jack Maguire,
> *Dhammapada: Annotated & Explained*, p. 3)

If you live for pleasures only—
uncontrolled sensually, immoderate in diet, idle, and weak—
evil will surely overthrow you,
as the wind blows down a feeble tree.
But if you do not live for pleasures only—
well-controlled sensually, moderate in diet, diligent, and strong—
this one evil will surely not overthrow,
any more than the wind blows down a mountain of stone.

> (Dhammapada 7–8; Max Müller, trans., revised by Jack Maguire,
> *Dhammapada: Annotated & Explained*, p. 3)

Evildoers mourn in this world and the next.
They mourn in both.
They mourn and grieve
when they see the filthiness of their own deeds.
Virtuous ones delight in this world
and delight in the next one.
They delight in both.
They delight and rejoice
when they see the purity of their own deeds.

> (Dhammapada 15–16; Max Müller, trans., revised by Jack Maguire,
> *Dhammapada: Annotated & Explained*, p. 5)

Evildoers suffer in this world and in the next.
They suffer in both.
They suffer
when they think of the evil they have done.
They suffer even more
when they continue on the evil path.
Virtuous ones are happy in this world
and in the next.
They are happy
when they think of the good they have done.
They are even happier
when they continue on the good path.

> (Dhammapada 17–18; Max Müller, trans., revised by Jack Maguire,
> *Dhammapada: Annotated & Explained*, p. 5)

Thoughtless ones,
even if they can recite many sacred verses
but do not follow them,
have no claim to a religious life,
but are like cowherders counting the cows of others.

Thoughtful ones,
even if they can recite only a few verses
but do follow the law and,
forsaking lust, hatred, and delusion,
possess true knowledge and peace of mind—
they, clinging to nothing in this world or the next,
have indeed a claim to a religious life.

> (Dhammapada 19–20; Max Müller, trans., revised by Jack Maguire,
> *Dhammapada: Annotated & Explained*, pp. 5, 7)

If you encounter someone who is intelligent,
shows you what is to be avoided,
and gives reproof where it is due,
follow that wise person as you would
someone who reveals hidden treasures.
It will be better, not worse, for you.
Let this wise one admonish, teach,
and forbid what is improper.
Such a person will be loved by the good
and hated by the bad.

> (Dhammapada 76–77; Max Müller, trans., revised by Jack Maguire,
> *Dhammapada: Annotated & Explained*, p. 27)

Do not have evildoers or low people for friends.
Have virtuous people for friends.
Have for friends the best of people.

> (Dhammapada 78; Max Müller, trans., revised by Jack Maguire,
> *Dhammapada: Annotated & Explained*, p. 27)

One whose friends are unreliable
soon comes to ruin.
But there is a friend
who is closer than a sibling.

> (Proverbs 18:24)

Do not befriend the hot-tempered
nor associate with the angry,
for you mimic them and become entrapped.
  (Proverbs 22:24–25; *Proverbs: Annotated & Explained*, p. 161)

There is no greater love
than the love that is willing to die for friends.
  (John 15:13)

As iron sharpens iron,
so a friend sharpens a friend.
  (Proverbs 27:17; *Proverbs: Annotated & Explained*, p. 201)

To have a friend is better than to be alone.
Together they enhance their labor,
and if one falls, the other assists.
How sad to fall alone, with none to raise you!
If two share a single bed
each will keep the other warm.
For how does one who sleeps alone stay warm?
Though one may be overpowered,
two can withstand the attack.
And a threefold friendship is stronger still.
  (Ecclesiastes 4:9–12; *Ecclesiastes: Annotated & Explained*, pp. 41, 43)

Yehoshua ben Perachyah teaches,
Make yourself worthy of a teacher,
secure for yourself a friend,
and judge everyone favorably.
  (*Pirke Avot* 1:6; *Ethics of the Sages: Pirke Avot—Annotated & Explained*, p. 9)

Be vigorous in doing good.
Take pains not to do evil.
If you do what is good slothfully,
your mind can easily and eagerly
turn toward evil thoughts.

> (Dhammapada 116; Max Müller, trans., revised by Jack Maguire,
> *Dhammapada: Annotated & Explained*, p. 39)

Turn from evil and do good.
Seek peace and pursue peace.

> (Psalm 34:14)

Sin is natural to this world
and you will not suffer punishment from it in the world to come.
Punishment is earned not from sinning
but from failing to repent when a sin in committed.
While the power to resist sin was not given,
the power to repent sin was given.
If you would merit God's mercy—repent.
If you would merit God's wrath—do not.
Yet do not imagine God is angry with you.
God is only angry with the evil you do
and of which you refuse to repent.
While people speak of God as passionate and vengeful,
these are only projections of our own minds.
Though people imagine otherwise,
the God they see is but a reflection of themselves.
God is beyond all such things.

> (Saint Theognostos II, "On the Practice of the Virtues," sec. 47; *Philokalia*)

From that time on
Jesus began to preach:
"Repent, for the kingdom is near."
    (Matthew 4:17)

If you commit a sin,
do not commit the same sin again.
Take no delight in evil:
The accumulation of evil is painful.
If you do what is good,
do the same thing again.
Take delight in good:
The accumulation of good is joyful.
    (Dhammapada 117–118; Max Müller, trans., revised by Jack Maguire,
    Dhammapada: Annotated & Explained, p. 39)

Don't think lightly of evil, saying inwardly,
"This will not bring me sorrow."
Even by the falling of tiny water drops,
a water pot is filled.
Fools become full of evil,
even if they gather it little by little.
Don't think lightly of good, saying inwardly,
"This will not bring me happiness."
Even by the falling of tiny water drops,
a water pot is filled.
Wise ones become full of good,
even if they gather it little by little.
    (Dhammapada 121–122; Max Müller, trans., revised by Jack Maguire,
    Dhammapada: Annotated & Explained, p. 39)

Do not obey evil laws!
Do not live on in thoughtlessness!

Do not follow false doctrines!
Do not be enamored of the world!
Rouse yourself!
Do not be idle!
Follow the law of virtue!
The virtuous rest in bliss
in this world and the next.

> (Dhammapada 167–169; Max Müller, trans., revised by Jack Maguire,
> *Dhammapada: Annotated & Explained*, p. 55)

To know the right thing to do,
and yet not to do it,
this is sin.

> (James 4:17)

After all has been heard,
the end of the matter is this:
Regarding reality—wonder!
Regarding right living—diligence!
This is true for everyone.

> (Ecclesiastes 12:13; *Ecclesiastes: Annotated & Explained*, p. 111)

One who formerly was reckless
and afterward became sober
brightens up this world
like the moon when freed from the clouds.
One whose evil deeds are covered by good deeds
brightens up this world
like the moon when freed from the clouds.

> (Dhammapada 172–173; Max Müller, trans., revised by Jack Maguire,
> *Dhammapada: Annotated & Explained*, p. 55)

I desire kindness,
not sacrifice;
knowledge of God,
rather than burnt offerings.

> (Hosea 6:6; *The Hebrew Prophets: Selections Annotated & Explained*, p. 49)

Not to commit any sin,
to do only good,
and to purify one's mind:
That is the teaching of all the awakened.

> (Dhammapada 183; Max Müller, trans., revised by Jack Maguire,
> *Dhammapada: Annotated & Explained*, p. 59)

Not to blame,
not to strike,
to live restrained under the law,
to be moderate in eating,
to sleep and sit alone,
and to dwell on the highest thoughts—
that is the teaching of the awakened.

> (Dhammapada 185; Max Müller, trans., revised by Jack Maguire,
> *Dhammapada: Annotated & Explained*, p. 59)

Patience is a sign of intelligence;
honor comes to those who do not take offense.

> (Proverbs 19:11; *Proverbs: Annotated & Explained*, p. 133)

If anger controls you,
sin awaits you.
Remain silent
and let your anger cool overnight.

> (Psalm 4:4)

Guard against anger of the body,
and control your body!
Cease committing sins of the body,
and practice goodness with your body.
Guard against anger of the tongue,
and control your tongue!
Cease committing sins of the tongue,
and practice goodness with your tongue.
Guard against anger of the mind,
and control your mind!
Cease committing sins of the mind,
and practice goodness with your mind.
The resolute who control body, tongue, and mind
are indeed well-controlled.

> (Dhammapada 231–234; Max Müller, trans., revised by Jack Maguire,
> *Dhammapada: Annotated & Explained*, p. 73)

Desist from anger.
Put away wrath.
Competing in anger leads to sin.

> (Psalm 37:8)

Resist evil with that which is superior to evil,
and your enemy will become a loyal and protecting friend.

> (Qur'an 41:34)

Have patience with those who slander you,
and take leave of them in a gentle manner.

> (Qur'an 73:10)

O you who have faith!
Spend on others out of the good things
that you may have acquired,
and out of that which We bring forth for you
out of the earth;
and do not choose for your spending
anything bad which you yourselves would not accept
without averting your eyes in disdain.
Know that God is the One Who is Rich,
the One Worthy of Praise.
Satan threatens you with the prospect of poverty
and bids you to be stingy,
while God promises you forgiveness and abundance;
God is infinite, all-knowing,
granting wisdom to whom God wills:
and whoever is granted wisdom
has indeed been granted abundant wealth.
Yet none bears this in mind
except those who are gifted with insight.

(Qur'an 2:267–9; Camille Helminski, trans., *The Light of Dawn:
Daily Readings from the Holy Qur'an*, p. 6)

The only true religion in the sight of God
is self-surrender to God.

(Qur'an 3:19; Camille Helminski, trans., *The Light of Dawn: Daily Readings
from the Holy Qur'an*, p. 9)

Never shall you attain righteousness
unless you spend on others
out of what you yourselves truly love;
and whatever you spend—certainly, God knows.

(Qur'an 3:92; Camille Helminski, trans., *The Light of Dawn: Daily Readings
from the Holy Qur'an*, p. 10)

And God does not grace with guidance
people who deliberately do wrong.
Those who have faith,
who have turned away from evil,
who strive hard in God's cause
with their possessions and their lives
have the highest rank in God's sight—
it is they who shall attain!
Their Sustainer gives them the glad tiding
of the grace that flows from God,
and of God's abundant acceptance,
and of the gardens which await them,
of enduring bliss,
there to dwell forever.
Truly, in God's Presence
is a mighty recompense!

> (Qur'an 9:19–22; Camille Helminski, trans., *The Light of Dawn:
> Daily Readings from the Holy Qur'an*, p. 39)

And do not touch the substance of orphans,
except to improve it, before they come of age.
And be true to every promise—
for, truly, you will be called to account for every promise
which you will have made!
And give full measure whenever you measure,
and weigh with a balance that is true:
this will be for your own good, and best in the end.
And never concern yourself
with anything of which you have no knowledge;
truly, hearing and sight and heart—all of them—
will be called to account for it!
And do not walk upon the earth with proud self-conceit:
for, truly, you can never rend the earth asunder,
nor can you ever grow as tall as the mountains!
The evil of all this is odious in your Sustainer's sight:

this is part of that knowledge of right and wrong
with which your Sustainer has inspired you.

>   (Qur'an 17:34–38; Camille Helminski, trans., *The Light of Dawn:
>   Daily Readings from the Holy Qur'an*, p. 66)

Defend the powerless and the orphan,
do justly by the oppressed and destitute.

>   (Psalm 82:3)

Grass-eaters do not mind changing pastures;
river creatures do not worry about changing waters.
They can make small changes without
ever losing their great constancy;
joy and anger, sadness and delight
do not enter into their breasts.
Now, in that they all live in the world,
the myriad things are one.
Realizing that they are ultimately
all part of overarching oneness,
their four limbs and hundred body parts
are just so much dust and dirt to them,
and all life and death, all beginning and end,
are just like the succession of day and night:
none of it can disturb them.
How much less will they be bothered
by the gain and loss, disaster and good fortune of ordinary life?

>   (Chuang-tzu 21; Livia Kohn, trans., *Chuang-tzu: The Tao of Perfect Happiness—
>   Selections Annotated & Explained*, p. 31)

There is no place
in the heavens above
or in the deepest waters below
where the moral law is not to be found.

>   (Confucius, *Doctrine of the Mean* 12)

Abba Anthony taught,
This is the great work of the spirit:
Repent continually before God.
Do not imagine you are without sin.
Sin is with you until you take your final breath.
Without sin there is no entering the Kingdom of Heaven.
Without sin there is no salvation.

(Anthony 4–5; *Apophthegmata Patrum* [Sayings of the Desert Fathers])

Abba Nilus said,
Do not long for things to go your way.
Long for them to go God's way.
In this you will be ever satisfied, calm, and grateful.

(Nilus 7; *Apophthegmata Patrum* [Sayings of the Desert Fathers])

Abba Poemen said,
The key to repentance?
Tears.
The key to virtue?
Tears.
There is no other way to God than this.

(Poemen 119; *Apophthegmata Patrum* [Sayings of the Desert Fathers])

My tears have been my food day and night.
(Psalm 42:3)

Even now, turn back to Me
with a whole heart, with fasting,
with weeping, and with lamentation.

Rend your heart and not your garment,
and return to Me.
I am gracious and kind,
patient and overflowing with compassion.
I renounce punishment.
Whoever knows, let them return and regret.

(Joel 2:12; *The Hebrew Prophets: Selections Annotated & Explained*, p. 69)

Abba Nisterus taught,
When you go to sleep at night
and when you awake in the morning
ask yourself this:
Where have I done that which is God's will?
And where have I avoided doing that which is not God's will?
Make this a lifelong practice.

(Nisterus 5; *Apophthegmata Patrum* [Sayings of the Desert Fathers])

Abba Nisterus said,
Devote each day to living rightly.
Pray each moment to be aware of God's presence,
for God is ever-present.
Take no refuge in rules or judgments.
Avoid harsh language, false testimony, and lies.
Don't get angry at other people, nor mock or ridicule them.
Do not imagine you are better than anyone—
for this above all results in tragedy.

(Nisterus 5; *Apophthegmata Patrum* [Sayings of the Desert Fathers])

Abba John said,
Make it a point each day
to cultivate even a bit of virtue.
Be patience and calm,

and devote body and soul to the love of God.
Be humble and have patience with your inner struggles.
Be watchful and pray diligently with awe and fervor.
Keep your speech kind and your senses controlled.
If others mock you, do not get angry, but stay calm.
Do not repay evil with evil.
Do not focus on the shortcomings of others,
nor compare yourself to them.
See yourself as less than even the most lowly of creatures.
Attach yourself to nothing of this world.

> (John the Dwarf 34; *Apophthegmata Patrum* [Sayings of the Desert Fathers])

Abba Poemen said,
Imagine meeting three people:
One of whom cultivates inner peace
even in times of strife;
one of whom cultivates inner gratitude
even in times of suffering;
and one of whom cultivates inner clarity
even in times of distraction.
Now know that you have met three people
doing the same spiritual work.

> (Poemen 29; *Apophthegmata Patrum* [Sayings of the Desert Fathers])

Be detached from your own welfare,
and impartial when considering others.
Do not stay silent when speech is called for,
nor abandon the world to hide in spirit.

> (Sirach 4:22–23; *The Divine Feminine in Biblical Wisdom Literature: Selections Annotated & Explained*, p. 133)

Do not speak too soon,
nor act too late.
Do not rule your household like a lion,
nor your servants like a watchdog.
Do not offer your palm in order to receive,
nor tighten your fist when it is time to give.

> (Sirach 4:29–31; *The Divine Feminine in Biblical Wisdom Literature:
> Selections Annotated & Explained*, p. 139)

If you are willing, you will be taught.
If you are diligent, you will progress.
If you listen, you will learn.
If you pay attention, you will become wise.

> (Sirach 6:32–33; *The Divine Feminine in Biblical Wisdom Literature:
> Selections Annotated & Explained*, p. 145)

Keep your attention on wisdom,
and do not allow yourself to be distracted.
Watch the patterns of creation.
This will enliven your soul
and bring you grace and tranquility.
Seeing truth you can walk forward in confidence
without stumbling because of ignorance.
When you sleep you will not be afraid;
your sleep will come easily.
When you wake you will not be anxious
nor worry about your fate,
for you rest safely in the Divine
and your feet do not stray from the path.

> (Proverbs 3:21–26; *Proverbs: Annotated & Explained*, p. 21)

Everything is beautiful in its moment,
but the ripening is hidden from your mind,
and you cannot comprehend beginnings or endings.
From this I concluded it is best for you
to rejoice in what is and devote your life to goodness.
This is the gift of reality:
eat and drink and find work that pleasures your heart.

    (Ecclesiastes 3:11–13; *Ecclesiastes: Annotated & Explained*, p. 31)

This is my guidance and the right path:
eat your bread with joy,
and drink your wine with gladness;
let your clothes be clean,
and let your head never lack for oil;
find a beloved with whom to share your life—
no matter how long or short.
This is what makes your life and your labor worthwhile.
Whatever falls into your hand to do,
do it without hesitation.
For in the grave there is neither doing,
nor reason, nor knowledge, nor wisdom.

    (Ecclesiastes 9:7–10; *Ecclesiastes: Annotated & Explained*, p. 85)

Jesus said,
Love your friend as your own soul.
Protect your friend as you would protect the pupil of your eye.

    (Gospel of Thomas 25; Stevan Davies, trans., *The Gospel of Thomas:
Annotated & Explained*, p. 37)

Jesus said,
You see the splinter in your friend's eye,
but you do not see the log in your own eye.

Remove the log from your own eye,
and then you can clearly see to remove the splinter
from the eye of the other.

> (Gospel of Thomas 26; Stevan Davies, trans., *The Gospel of Thomas:
> Annotated & Explained*, p. 37)

Do not make a crutch of ego,
lean on God alone.
Adhere to the good and your path will be just.
Do not imagine that you are wise.
Know only that you do not know.
Stand in awe of the Infinite and turn away from evil.
In this way you strengthen both body and soul.
Know from Whom success comes
and give generously to those in need.
Your wealth will increase as a result of your generosity;
none can fathom the rewards of those
who share their wealth.
Not everything that happens will be enjoyable,
and not every word you hear will be kind,
yet receive everything as a gift and a teaching.

> (Proverbs 3:5–12 *Proverbs: Annotated & Explained*, p. 17)

Jesus said,
Do not worry
from morning to evening or evening to morning
about what you are going to wear.

> (Gospel of Thomas 36; Stevan Davies, trans., *The Gospel of Thomas:
> Annotated & Explained*, p. 47)

The Ineffable says:
Sow justice and reap compassion.
Make time to seek Me,

and I will come
and teach you the way of righteousness.
But ...
sow wickedness and reap iniquity,
and you will gag on the fruit of treachery.

(Hosea 10:12–13; *The Hebrew Prophets: Selections Annotated & Explained*, p. 95)

Don't fool yourself.
You can't make a fool out of God.
Whatever grows in your garden
is going to be what you planted there.
If you plant Flesh, then corruption is what will grow.
But if you plant Spirit, then life is what will grow.
So don't grow tired of doing what is right
because we will harvest what we've planted,
as long as we don't give up.

(Galatians 6:7–9; Ron Miller, trans., *The Sacred Writings of Paul: Annotated & Explained*, p. 79)

You shouldn't owe anything to anyone except love.
When you love someone, you have fulfilled the Teaching.
The commandments—not to commit adultery,
not to murder, not to steal, not to covet,
and any other commandment—can all be summed up in one:
to love your neighbor as yourself.
Since love never wrongs the neighbor,
love fulfills the Teaching.

(Romans 13:8–10; Ron Miller, trans., *The Sacred Writings of Paul: Annotated & Explained*, p. 139)

My brothers and sisters,
you are being called to freedom.
Make sure that you don't use this freedom

as license for the Flesh.

Serve one another in love.

For the entire Teaching can be understood in this:

Love your neighbor as yourself.

> (Galatians 5:13–14; Ron Miller, trans., *The Sacred Writings of Paul: Annotated & Explained*, p. 143)

Rabbi Hillel taught,

That which is hateful to you do not do to another.

This is the whole of the Teaching.

All the rest is commentary.

Now go and study it.

> (Babylonian Talmud, *Shabbat* 31a)

Jesus said,

Love the Ineffable with all your heart,

with all your breath,

with all you have and are,

and love your neighbor as yourself—

this is the whole of the Teaching and the Prophets.

> (Matthew 22:37–40)

It is not [the mark of] righteousness

that you turn your faces toward east or west.

Rather, truly righteous are those who

believe in God and the last day,

and the angels and the scriptures,

and the prophets;

and who give material gifts out of love for God,

even of what they care for,

to relatives and orphans,

and the poor and the traveler and the needy,

and for the freeing of slaves;

and who establish prayer and give alms;

and who fulfill their promises which they have made;

and those who are patient in misfortune, affliction, and hardship—

such are the people of truth,

and they are the God-conscious ones.

> (Qur'an 2:177; Yusuf Ali, trans., revised by Sohaib N. Sultan *The Qur'an and Sayings of the Prophet Muhammad: Selections Annotated & Explained*, p. 59)

God will say,

O Human, I fell ill and you visited Me not.

And you will say,

O God, how can I visit You

when You are the God of the worlds?

God will say,

You knew one had fallen ill

and yet you did not visit.

Did you not know that had you visited

you would have found Me there as well?

God will say,

O Human, I asked for food and you refused.

And you will say,

O God, how can I feed You

when You are the God of the worlds?

God will say,

You knew one who asked you for food

and yet you refused.

Did you not know that had you offered food

you would surely have found Me there?

God will say,

O Human,

I asked for water and you refused.

And you will say,

O God, how can I give You water

when You are the God of the worlds?

God will say,

You knew one who asked you for water, and you refused.

Had you not refused

you would have surely found Me there.

> (Hadith of the Prophet Muhammad; Yusuf Ali, trans., revised by Sohaib N.
> Sultan, *The Qur'an and Sayings of the Prophet Muhammad: Selections Annotated
> & Explained*, p. 61)

Men should not mock other men,

for these may be better than they are.

And women should not mock other women,

for these may be better than they are.

And do not ridicule each other

or call each other by insulting nicknames.

Evil is the name of impiety after achieving faith;

and they who do not refrain are wrongdoers.

Avoid suspicion, for suspicion is sin,

and do not spy on each other,

and do not defame each other in their absence.

> (Qur'an 49:11–12; Yusuf Ali, trans., revised by Sohaib N. Sultan,
> *The Qur'an and Sayings of the Prophet Muhammad: Selections Annotated &
> Explained*, p. 109)

Be good, as God has been good to you,

and seek not mischief in the land,

for God loves not those who do mischief.

> (Qur'an 28:77; Yusuf Ali, trans., revised by Sohaib N. Sultan, *The Qur'an
> and Sayings of the Prophet Muhammad: Selections Annotated & Explained*, p. 121)

I give you a new instruction:

Love one another.

As I have loved you,

so you must love one another.

> (John 13:34)

God has decreed that
you worship none other than God,
and that you be kind to parents.
Whether one or both of them attain old age in your lifetime,
say not to them a word of contempt, nor repel them,
but address them in an honorable manner.
And, out of compassion, lower to them [your] wings of humility,
and say,
"My Lord! Bestow on them your Mercy
as they cherished me when I was young."

> (Qur'an 17:23–24; Yusuf Ali, trans., revised by Sohaib N. Sultan,
> *The Qur'an and Sayings of the Prophet Muhammad: Selections Annotated &*
> *Explained*, p. 123)

Honor your father and your mother.

> (Exodus 20:12)

Cover not truth with falsehood,
nor conceal the truth when you know what it is.

> (Qur'an 2:42; Yusuf Ali, trans., revised by Sohaib N. Sultan, *The Qur'an*
> *and Sayings of the Prophet Muhammad: Selections Annotated & Explained*,
> p. 127)

Do not lie. Do not deceive one another.

> (Leviticus 19:11)

Persevere, excel in patience, and be constant.
Be conscious of God so that you may be successful.

> (Qur'an 3:200; Yusuf Ali, trans., revised by Sohaib N. Sultan, *The Qur'an*
> *and Sayings of the Prophet Muhammad: Selections Annotated & Explained*,
> p. 127)

The righteous are those who
give generously in times of ease and difficulty,
who control their anger,
and who are forgiving toward people.
Surely God loves those who do good.

> (Qur'an 3:134; Yusuf Ali, trans., revised by Sohaib N. Sultan, *The Qur'an and Sayings of the Prophet Muhammad: Selections Annotated & Explained*, p. 127)

And swell not your cheek out of pride,
nor walk in insolence through the earth;
for God loves not any arrogant boaster.

> (Qur'an 31:18; Yusuf Ali, trans., revised by Sohaib N. Sultan, *The Qur'an and Sayings of the Prophet Muhammad: Selections Annotated & Explained*, p. 127)

We live happily indeed when
we are not hating those who hate us!
Among those who hate us
let us dwell free from hatred!
We live happily indeed
when we are free from ailments among the ailing!
Among those who are ailing
let us dwell free from ailments!
We live happily indeed
when we are free from greed among the greedy!
Among those who are greedy
let us dwell free from greed!
We live happily indeed
when we call nothing our own!
We shall be like the bright gods, feeding on happiness!
Victory breeds hatred, for the conquered are unhappy.

Those who have given up both victory and defeat
are content and happy.

> (Dhammapada 197–201; Max Müller, trans., revised by Jack Maguire,
> *Dhammapada: Annotated & Explained*, p. 63)

One who walks in the company of fools suffers a long way.
Company with fools, as with enemies, is always painful.
Company with the wise is happiness, like meeting with family.
Therefore one ought to follow the wise,
the intelligent, the learned, the much-enduring, the dutiful, the
   worthy.
One ought to follow the good and the wise,
as the moon follows the path of the stars.

> (Dhammapada 207–208; Max Müller, trans., revised by Jack Maguire,
> *Dhammapada: Annotated & Explained*, p. 65)

Yose ben Yoezer taught,
Make your home a meeting place for the wise;
sit in the dust of their feet,
and drink in their wisdom thirstily.

> (*Pirke Avot* 1:4, *Ethics of the Sages: Pirke Avot—Annotated & Explained*, p. 7)

In this world, is there such a thing as perfect happiness?
To attain wealth,
people submit to great suffering
and make themselves sick.
Then they accumulate so much stuff
that they cannot even use it!
However dedicated they are to their lives,
it is yet entirely outside of themselves.
To attain position, people slave day and night
without stopping.
Even then, they keep worrying constantly

whether they come across as being good at their job!
However dedicated they are to their lives,
it is yet entirely separate from them.
When people are born, whatever they do,
frustration is born along with them.
Thus, even to attain long life,
people make themselves ignorant and dull.
Still, they spend all their time worrying about not dying.
However dedicated they are to their lives,
it is yet far away from them.

> (Chuang-tzu 18; Livia Kohn, trans., *Chuang-tzu: The Tao of Perfect Happiness—Selections Annotated & Explained*, pp. 3, 5)

Is there in fact happiness?
Is it possible in this life and world?
To me it is found only in complete noncoercive action,
something that ordinary people see as great suffering.
Thus the saying:
"Perfect happiness is being free
from the need to be happy.
Perfect accomplishment is being free
from having to accomplish anything."
What is right and wrong in the world
is impossible to decide.
However, in noncoercive action there is
clear right and wrong.
Perfect happiness and living to the fullest
can only be realized in this state of noncoercive action.

> (Chuang-tzu 18; Livia Kohn, trans., *Chuang-tzu: The Tao of Perfect Happiness—Selections Annotated & Explained*, p. 7)

Amassing material goods,
the wealthy try to find comfort.
Amassing power and influence,

they try to find fulfillment.
Resting quietly for a moment,
they sink into depression.
Engaging themselves physically,
they turn into maniacs—this is sickness.
Pursuing wealth and running after profit,
they fill their houses to overflowing
and do not know how to escape.
Still, they lust for more and cannot resist—this is addiction.
More stuff piled up than they could ever use,
grasping for more than they could ever hold,
their mind is full of care and close to exhaustion,
yet they still keep going after projects and things,
not knowing when to stop—this is trouble.
At home suspicious of theft by deceitful servants,
in town terrified of attacks by robbers and con artists,
they surround themselves with defenses
and dare not walk around by themselves outside—this is fear.
Sickness, addiction, trouble, and fear—
these are among the greatest evils in the world.

   (Chuang-tzu 29; Livia Kohn, trans., *Chuang-tzu: The Tao of Perfect Happiness—
   Selections Annotated & Explained*, p. 11)

Hillel used to say,
The more fat, the more disease.
The more possessions, the more worry.
The more wives, the more rivalry.
The more maids, the more frivolity.
The more butlers, the more theft.
However, the more Wisdom, the more life.
The more study, the more wisdom.
The more guidance, the more understanding.
The more generosity, the more peace.
A good reputation will serve you in this world;
knowledge of Wisdom will serve you in the next.

   (*Pirke Avot* 2:8; *Ethics of the Sages: Pirke Avot—Annotated & Explained*, p. 25)

What can you show for all your effort?
What value do you glean from your worrisome preoccupations?
Dissatisfaction arises daily,
and business is a frustration so great that your mind cannot sleep at
    night.
To live this way is absurd!
So what isn't absurd?
To eat simply, and drink moderately,
and do work that satisfies the soul.
This is what reality offers us.

(Ecclesiastes 2:22–24; *Ecclesiastes: Annotated & Explained*, p. 23)

The Ineffable says:
Do I need your endless sacrifices?
I am stuffed with burnt offerings.
I cannot stand your pomp and solemnity.
I am disgusted by your ceremonies of time and season.
Wash yourselves clean, put away your evil acts,
cease from doing evil, learn to do good.
Seek justice, aid the wronged,
defend the powerless, the orphan, and the widow.
Come, let us reason together.
Even if your sins are scarlet,
they can become snow white;
even if they are as wool dyed crimson,
they can be white as fleece.

(Isaiah 1:11–19; *The Hebrew Prophets: Selections Annotated & Explained*, p. 77)

The Ineffable says:
I hate your holy days
and despise your festivals;
I am not moved by your solemn gatherings.

Your offerings are rejected;
I ignore your slaughtered gifts.
Spare me the sound of your hymns,
and let the music of your lutes fall silent;
I am not listening.
Rather let justice well up like water,
let righteousness flow like a mighty stream.

> (Amos 5:21–24; *The Hebrew Prophets: Selections Annotated & Explained*, p. 105)

I created invisible spirits and human beings
only to worship and serve Me.
No sustenance do I require of them,
nor do I require that they should feed Me,
for it is God, the Source of all might,
who gives sustenance.

> (Qur'an 51:56–58; Yusuf Ali, trans., revised by Sohaib N. Sultan, *The Qur'an
> and Sayings of the Prophet Muhammad: Selections Annotated & Explained*, p. 57)

The Ineffable says:
Execute true justice;
deal kindly and compassionately with one another.
Do not oppress the widow, the orphan, the stranger, and the poor.
Do not set your heart to plotting evil.

> (Zechariah 7:8–10; *The Hebrew Prophets: Selections Annotated & Explained*,
> p. 111)

The Ineffable says:
Beat your swords into plowshares
and your spears into pruning knives.
Do not lift up sword nation against nation;
nor study war anymore.
Rather sit under your vine and your fig tree,
and be unafraid.

> (Micah 4:3–4; *The Hebrew Prophets: Selections Annotated & Explained*, p. 155)

O you who believe,

stand out firmly for justice, as witnesses to God,

even against yourselves, or your parents, or your siblings,

and whether it be against rich or poor,

for God can best protect both.

Follow not your lusts, lest you swerve,

and if you distort or decline to do justice,

verily God is all acquainted with all that you do.

> (Qur'an 4:135; Yusuf Ali, trans., revised by Sohaib N. Sultan, *The Qur'an and Sayings of the Prophet Muhammad: Selections Annotated & Explained*, p. 157)

O you who believe,

stand out firmly for God, as witnesses to fairness,

and let not the hatred of others cause you

to swerve toward wrong and depart from justice.

Be just, that is closer to piety,

and be conscious of God,

for God is well-acquainted with all that you do.

> (Qur'an 5:8; Yusuf Ali, trans., revised by Sohaib N. Sultan, *The Qur'an and Sayings of the Prophet Muhammad: Selections Annotated & Explained*, p. 159)

God commands justice,

the doing of good, and giving to others;

and God forbids all shameful deeds, injustice, and oppression.

God instructs you so that you may be mindful.

> (Qur'an 16:90; Yusuf Ali, trans., revised by Sohaib N. Sultan, *The Qur'an and Sayings of the Prophet Muhammad: Selections Annotated & Explained*, p. 157)

Come, let me convey to you

what God has prohibited:

Do not attribute divinity, in any way, to anything beside God;

be good to your parents;
and do not kill your children out of fear of poverty—
for it is We who shall provide sustenance
for you as well as for them;
and do not incline towards any shameful deeds,
whether openly or in secret;
and do not take the life of a single soul—
which God has declared sacred—
except out of justice: this has the One instructed you
that you might learn wisdom.
And do not touch the substance of orphans—
except to improve it—before they come of age.
And give full measure and weigh equitably:
no burden do We place on any soul,
but that which it can bear;
and when you speak, speak justly,
even if a near relative is concerned;
and always observe your bond with God:
this has God asked of you, that you might remember.
And this is the way leading straight to Me:
follow it, then, and do not follow other ways,
that they might not cause you to wander from God's way.
This has God asked of you,
so that you might remain conscious of God.

> (Qur'an 6:151–153; Camille Helminski, trans., *The Light of Dawn: Daily Readings from the Holy Qur'an*, p. 30)

If you do good,
your reward is better than your deed;
but if you do harm,
your punishment is only to the extent of your deed.

> (Qur'an 28:84; Camille Helminski, trans., *The Light of Dawn: Daily Readings from the Holy Qur'an*, p. 100)

Abba Poemen said,
Water is soft.
Stone is hard.
Yet if left to drip on the stone long enough
the soft will overcome the hard.
The word of God is soft.
The human heart is hard.
Yet as with water and stone,
the word will soften the heart
if allowed to drip upon it long enough.

(Poemen 183; *Apophthegmata Patrum* [Sayings of the Desert Fathers])

Abba Poemen said,
Discipline your mouth
to speak what is in your heart.

(Poemen 164; *Apophthegmata Patrum* [Sayings of the Desert Fathers])

With generosity and kind words
always doing to others what is good,
treat all people as the same.

(Anguttara Nikyaya)

You are made in the image of God [Genesis 1:27]
so be nothing less than godly.
In this you are honoring
the gift of God's presence and peace.

(Saint Maximos the Confessor II, "First Century of Various Texts," sec. 28;
Philokalia)

CHAPTER EIGHT

Dying Wisely

Returning to the One

What you imagine happens to you after you die depends on who you imagine you are while you are alive. If, for example, you believe you are a soul inhabiting a body, you may believe that your soul survives the death of that body. And if this is your belief, you may also believe that the soul has its own fate after the body's death: heaven or hell or reincarnation, for example. And if you believe in an afterlife or reincarnation, you must also believe in some criteria for determining who merits heaven and who merits hell, or who incarnates in a higher station and who in a lower.

If, on the other hand, you believe that you are the body only, you may believe that when the body dies, you die as well, and all talk of life after life is simply a ploy to earn your allegiance to one system of belief or another, depending on which offers you the better afterlife scenario.

In either case, what you believe about the afterlife is conditioned by what you believe about this life.

Perennial wisdom offers a third alternative: you are neither a being separate from the body nor a being limited to the body but *being* itself manifesting body and mind the way an ocean manifests waves. When the body dies, the mind dies, but *being* continues—not your finite egoic being, but infinite and dynamic *being* itself, Ultimate Reality, the Self your self knows itself to be when cleansed of the optical delusion of separateness: the birthless and deathless Eternal I that is the *you* you are when stripped of the *you* you imagine yourself to be.

Imagine tying a knot in a foot-long piece of cotton rope. What is the relationship between the knot and the rope? While identifiable as a distinct knot, the knot is not other than the rope; it is simply the rope in a unique configuration. The rope is not any less or any more than what it was before you tied the knot. Nothing essential has changed.

Now imagine tying a second knot in the rope. Comparing one knot to the other you find that each is distinct and unique, and yet both are nothing but the same rope. What is true of knots on a rope is true of your being and of *being* itself. The knot is the self, the ego, your personality. The rope is Ultimate Reality, the Eternal I, and the Self. Death is the untying of the knot of self, but the rope itself remains. The extent to which you identify with the knot is the extent to which you wonder (if not worry) about an afterlife or lack thereof. The extent to which you identify as the rope is the extent to which the question of an afterlife is moot.

Perennial wisdom does not deny the reality of death; it simply teaches that every being is a temporary manifestation of *being*—Ultimate Reality. Perennial wisdom allows you to grieve over the death of a loved one but not to worry about the fate of any one, for every one is an expression of the only One from which and in which one-ness arises and to which it returns.

At the end of an era all creatures disintegrate into my nature
and at the beginning of another era I manifest them again.
Such is my nature:
to follow again and again
the pattern of the Infinite manifestations and disintegrations.
   (Bhagavad Gita 9:7–8; Shri Purohit Swami, trans., *Bhagavad Gita: Annotated & Explained*, p. 71)

There was never a time when I was not,
nor you, nor these princes were not;
there will never be a time when we shall cease to be.
   (Bhagavad Gita 2:12; Shri Purohit Swami, trans., *Bhagavad Gita: Annotated & Explained*, p. 13)

That which is not, shall never be;

that which is, shall never cease to be.

To the wise, these truths are self-evident.

The Spirit, which pervades all that we see, is imperishable.

Nothing can destroy the Spirit.

> (Bhagavad Gita 2:16–17; Shri Purohit Swami, trans., *Bhagavad Gita:*
> *Annotated & Explained*, p. 13)

It was not born; It will never die:

nor once having been, can It ever cease to be:

Unborn, Eternal, Ever-Enduring, yet Most Ancient,

the Spirit dies not when the body is dead.

You who know the Spirit are

Indestructible, Immortal, Unborn, Always-the-Same.

As you discard threadbare robes and put on new,

so the Spirit throws off Its worn-out bodies and takes fresh ones.

Weapons cleave It not, fire burns It not,

water drenches It not, and wind dries It not.

It is impenetrable;

It can be neither drowned nor scorched nor dried.

It is Eternal, All-Pervading, Unchanging, Immovable, and Most Ancient.

It is named the Unmanifest, the Unthinkable, the Immutable.

Wherefore, knowing the Spirit as such, you have no cause to grieve.

> (Bhagavad Gita 2:20–25; Shri Purohit Swami, trans., *Bhagavad Gita:*
> *Annotated & Explained*, p. 15)

Seeking to console Chuang-tzu on the death of his wife

Hui Shih visited and found him

singing and drumming on pots.

"How unfeeling!" Hui Shih cried.

Chuang-tzu replied,

 "At first, I could not stop crying.

Then I examined the matter from the very beginning.

At the very beginning, she was not living,

having no form, nor even substance.
But somehow there was then her substance,
then her form, and then her life.
Now by a further change, she has died.
The whole process is like the sequence of the four seasons,
spring, summer, autumn, and winter.
For me to go about weeping and wailing
would be to proclaim myself ignorant of the natural laws.
Therefore I stopped!"
   (Chuang-tzu18)

It is We Who give life and who give death:
It is We Who remain after all else passes away.
   (Qur'an 15:19; Camille Helminski, trans., *The Light of Dawn: Daily Readings from the Holy Qur'an*, p. 57)

All the flourishing things will return to their source.
This return is peaceful; it is the flow of nature,
An eternal decay and renewal.
   (Tao Te Ching 16)

There is no destruction, either in this world or in the next.
No evil fate awaits those who tread the path of righteousness.
Having reached the worlds where the righteous dwell,
and having remained there for many years,
you will be born again
and strive for perfection more eagerly than before.
Then, after many lives,
you attain perfection and reach the Supreme.
   (Bhagavad Gita 6:40–45; Shri Purohit Swami, trans., *Bhagavad Gita: Annotated & Explained*, p. 57)

If at the time of your death you think only of Me,

and thinking thus leave the body and go forth,

assuredly you will know Me.

Wherever your mind fixates at the moment of death,

there you will go.

Therefore meditate on Me always,

for if mind and reason are fixed on Me,

to Me you shall surely come.

> (Bhagavad Gita 8:5–7; Shri Purohit Swami, trans., *Bhagavad Gita: Annotated & Explained*, p. 65)

If your mind does not wander,

and you are engaged in constant meditation,

you will attain the Supreme Spirit.

If you meditate on Me, the Omniscient, the Ancient,

who is more minute than the atom,

and yet the Ruler and Upholder of all,

Unimaginable, Brilliant like the Sun,

beyond the reach of darkness,

to Me you shall surely come.

If you leave the body with mind unmoved and filled with devotion,

by the power of your meditation you attain the Supreme.

> (Bhagavad Gita 8:8–10; Shri Purohit Swami, trans., *Bhagavad Gita: Annotated & Explained*, pp. 65, 67)

As the gates of your body close,

draw the forces of your mind into the heart

and concentrate on Me.

Repeating Om, the Symbol of Eternity,

holding Me always in remembrance,

you will leave your body and go forth to the Spirit Supreme.

For to those who constantly think of Me and Me alone,

I am always accessible.

> (Bhagavad Gita 8:12–13; Shri Purohit Swami, trans., *Bhagavad Gita: Annotated & Explained*, p. 67)

Coming thus to Me,
you are free from misery and death,
and have gained perfection.
While the entirety of creation continues
the cycle of birth, death, and rebirth,
for those who come to Me there is no rebirth.

> (Bhagavad Gita 8:15–16; Shri Purohit Swami, trans., *Bhagavad Gita:*
> *Annotated & Explained*, p. 67)

Not in the sky, not in the sea, not in the clefts of the mountain
is there known a spot in the whole world
where one might live free from being overcome by death.

> (Dhammapada 128; Max Müller, trans., revised by Jack Maguire,
> *Dhammapada: Annotated & Explained*, p. 41)

Amma Sarah said,
Before my foot shifts from one rung to the next
my eyes focus solely on death.

> (Sarah 6; *Apophthegmata Patrum* [Sayings of the Desert Fathers])

Abba Evagrius said,
Take refuge in your cell.
Gather your thoughts.
Imagine your death.
Feel the body's end,
experience the sorrow and the suffering,
and free yourself from clinging to this world.
Knowing what it is to die
you are free to live in peace.

> (Evagrius 1; *Apophthegmata Patrum* [Sayings of the Desert Fathers])

Abba Rufus said,
Stay mindful of your mortality.
Know that death may befall you at any moment.
In this way you will protect your soul from the snare of certainty.

    (Rufus 1; *Apophthegmata Patrum* [Sayings of the Desert Fathers])

It is more advantageous to visit
a house of mourning than a house of feasting;
for death is our common end,
and only a heart at home with death truly lives.
Grief is preferable to gaiety,
bringing a reflective sorrow that awakens compassion.
Thus the heart of the wise rests in the home of sorrow,
while the heart of the fool clings to the house of feasting.

    (Ecclesiastes 7:2–4; *Ecclesiastes: Annotated & Explained*, p. 61.)

Blessed are those who mourn
for they will be comforted.

    (Matthew 5:4)

Abba Benjamin taught from his deathbed,
Three things will bring you salvation:
Cultivate joy regardless of the situation.
Keep your prayer constant and undistracted.
Be grateful for all you receive, wanted and unwanted.

    (Benjamin 4; *Apophthegmata Patrum* [Sayings of the Desert Fathers])

The disciples asked Jesus:
Tell us about our end.
What will it be?
Jesus replied:
Have you found the Beginning
so that you now seek the end?
The place of the Beginning will be the place of the end.
Blessed is anyone who will
stand up in the Beginning
and thereby know the end and never die.

>   (Gospel of Thomas 18a–b; Stevan Davies, trans., *The Gospel of Thomas:
>   Annotated & Explained*, p. 25)

Life is the follower of death,
and death is the beginning of life—
who knows their inherent structure?
Human life is nothing but an assemblance of vital energy.
When it comes together, we come to life;
when it scatters, we die.
Since life and death thus closely follow each other,
why whine about either?
In this most essential aspect, the myriad things are one.
They consider life as beautiful
because it is spiritual and marvelous;
they think of death as nasty
because it is smelly and putrid.
However, the smelly and putrid change again
and become the spiritual and marvelous;
the spiritual and marvelous change once more
and turn smelly and putrid.
Thus the saying: "The entire world is but one vital energy."
Based on this, all sages value oneness.

>   (Chuang-tzu 22; Livia Kohn, trans., *Chuang-tzu: The Tao of Perfect Happiness—
>   Selections Annotated & Explained*, p. 33)

Even if you think of [the One]
as constantly being born, and constantly dying;
even then you still have no cause to grieve.

> (Bhagavad Gita 2:26–28; Shri Purohit Swami, trans., *Bhagavad Gita:
> Annotated & Explained*, p. 15)

Happy are you whose hour of death
reflects your hour of birth.
Just as you were pure
as you entered this world,
so may you be pure as you depart from it.

> (Rabbi Berekhiah, Jerusalem Talmud, *Megillah* 1:9:8L)

Rabbi Eliezer said,
"Repent the day before you die."
His students asked,
"Since we cannot know the day of our death,
how can we know upon which day to repent?"
Rabbi Eliezer replied,
"Then repent today,
and spend each day doing the same."

> (*Avot de Rabbi Nathan* 15:4)

Warnings from the Dark Side

Scriptures of Hate, Fear, and Violence

The World Wisdom Bible focuses on texts that reflect perennial wisdom. In so doing we might give the impression that the scriptures from which these texts are drawn reflect in their entirety perennial wisdom as well. They do not. While these scriptures contain the teachings of perennial wisdom, they also contain a much larger body of teaching that is highly parochial as well as often xenophobic and violent.

While *The World Wisdom Bible* is rich with "love your neighbor" and "love the stranger" (Leviticus 19:18, 19:34), there is no dearth of texts in the world's religions demanding we "show them no mercy" (Deuteronomy 7:2). Human evil is no less perennial than human good and often speaks with the same religious authority as the good. We include some of these darker texts here as warnings: when you come across teachings such as these in the world's religions, know that they come not from the Self but the self, not from perennial wisdom but from the optical delusion that breeds fear, xenophobia, misogyny, and demonization of the other—values at odds with perennial wisdom's focus on unity, equality, compassion, justice, and the well-being of all beings as expressions of the one *being*, Ultimate Reality.

In presenting these texts, we remind ourselves of the universal human capacity for evil and how religion can be used to mask, excuse, and even promote it. By owning our capacity for evil, we are better prepared to free ourselves from it. By learning to recognize evil in our sacred texts, we are better equipped to resist the allure of doing evil in the name of some higher good.

When you draw near to wage war against a city,
first offer terms of surrender.
If they surrender, you may enslave all the inhabitants;
if they do not surrender, you may lay siege to the city,
and when YHVH your God gives the city over to you,
kill all the men.
You may, however,
take the women, children, livestock, and valuables as booty.
You may enjoy the spoils that YHVH your God has given you.
　　(Deuteronomy 20:10–14)

And kill the unbeliever wherever you find them
but do not fight them in the vicinity of the Ka'abah
unless they attack you there.
But if they do, then slay them,
for this is the reward of the unbeliever.
　　(Qur'an 2:191–192)

I remember what Amalek did to Israel,
the ambush they laid against the people
as they fled from Egypt.
Now go and strike down Amalek
and destroy all they have.
Have no pity on them—
kill man and woman alike, infant and nursling alike,
ox and sheep alike, camel and donkey alike.
　　(1 Samuel 15:2–3)

For death is as sure for that which is born
as birth is for that which is dead.
Therefore grieve not for what is inevitable.
The end and beginning of beings are unknown.

We see only the intervening formations,

then what cause is there for grief?

> (Bhagavad Gita 2:27–28; Shri Purohit Swami, trans., *Bhagavad Gita: Annotated & Explained*, p. 15)

The angel swung a sickle over the earth

and gathered in the unbelievers of the earth

and threw them into the great wine press of God's wrath.

And the wine press crushed those within it outside the city,

and blood flowed from the wine press

until it was as high as a horse's bridle

and as wide as two hundred miles.

> (Revelation 14:19–20)

You are obligated to fight even though you dislike it.

Isn't it possible that you dislike

that which is actually good for you,

even as you often love that which is bad for you?

Allah knows, and you do not.

> (Qur'an 2:244)

If you refuse to engage in this just war,

you reject your duty and earn dishonor and incur evil.

People will tell tales of your disgrace, a fate worse than death!

> (Bhagavad Gita 2:33–34; Shri Purohit Swami, trans., *Bhagavad Gita: Annotated & Explained*, p. 17)

Do not imagine I come to bring peace to the world;

not peace do I bring but the sword!

For I come to pit sons against fathers,

and daughters against mothers,

and daughters-in-law against mothers-in-law;
and your enemies will be members of your own household.
If you love your father or mother more than me
you are unworthy of me;
and if you love your son or daughter more than me
you are unworthy of me;
and if you do not take up the cross and follow me
you are not worthy of me.
Those who seek to protect their lives will lose them,
but those who lose their lives for my sake will find them.
   (Matthew 10:34–39)

If you come to me
and do not hate your father and mother,
wife and children, brothers and sisters,
indeed life itself,
you cannot be my disciple.
   (Luke 14:26)

One who blasphemes the name of YHVH
shall be put to death:
the entire community shall gather to stone the blasphemer.
Any who blasphemes, be they aliens or Israelites,
shall be put to death.
   (Leviticus 24:16)

Whoever refuses to seek YHVH
should be put to death, whether young or old, male or female.
   (2 Chronicles 15:13)

As to the unbelievers,
I will punish them with horrible terrors
in this world and in the Hereafter,
and there will be none to help them.

    (Qur'an 3:56)

Those who do not take refuge in Me
shall be as brittle branches gathered together
and cast into the fire that they might burn.

    (John 15:6)

Those who disbelieve in Our Revelations
shall surely burn in Hell.
And whenever their skin is consumed by the flames
We shall give them new skins
so that their punishment never ceases.

    (Qur'an 4:56)

This is proof of God's righteous judgment
meant to make you worthy of God's kingdom
when the Lord Jesus is revealed from heaven
with his mighty angels in flaming fire
inflicting vengeance on those who did not know God
and on those who did not obey the gospel of our Lord Jesus.
These will suffer the punishment of eternal destruction.

    (2 Thessalonians 1:5–9)

Those who worship the beast and its image
and have a mark on their foreheads or hands
will drink the wine of God's anger
and suffer the torment of fire and sulfur

before the holy angels and in the presence of the Lamb.
And the smoke of their torture rises eternally.
There is no day of rest for them.

(Revelation 14:9–11)

Do not befriend those who reject Faith
until they flee from their unbelief
and follow the way of Allah.
But if they refuse the way of Allah
then grab them and kill them wherever you find them,
and make no friends or allies from among them.

(Qur'an 4:89)

Pass through the city and kill.
Let your eye spare no one,
and show no mercy.
Slaughter old men and young men
and young women, children and women.

(Ezekiel 9:5–6)

If you have no pride,
and your intellect is unalloyed by attachment,
even though you slaughter these people
you do not kill them, and your act does not bind you.

(Bhagavad Gita 18:17; Shri Purohit Swami, trans., *Bhagavad Gita: Annotated & Explained*, p. 139)

The Israelites battled against Midian
as YHVH had commanded Moses
and they killed every male.
The Israelites enslaved

the women and their children;
and they took the cattle and sheep
and all they owned as spoils of war.
They set their towns and settlements aflame,
but took for themselves the spoils, both people and animals.
The commanders brought the captives and the spoils to Moses.
Moses grew angry with them saying,
"You spared the lives of the women
who seduced the Israelites to act against YHVH?
Now kill every boy child,
and kill every woman who is not a virgin.
But all the young virgins you may keep for yourselves."
    (Numbers 31:7–18)

The punishment of those who wage war
against God and God's messenger,
and who seek to do evil in the land is this:
they shall be killed or crucified,
or their hands and feet should be cut off from opposite sides,
or they shall be banished from the land.
    (Qur'an 5:33)

Any who cause one of these little ones—
those who believe in me—to stumble,
it would be better for them
to drown in the sea
with a grinding stone hung around their neck.
If your hand causes you to stumble—cut it off!
Better to live maimed
than to go intact into the unquenchable fires of hell.
If your foot causes you to stumble—cut it off!
Better for you to live crippled
than to be thrown intact into hell.

If your eye causes you to stumble—pluck it out!
Better for you to enter the kingdom of God
with one eye than to enter hell with two,
where the worms consume you endlessly,
and the fire is never quenched.
   (Mark 9:42–48)

Let Your enemies be drenched in burning coals;
let them be thrown into fiery pits so deep
that they cannot climb out again.
   (Psalm 140:10)

Those in Hell will yearn to escape the Fire
but there is no escape.
Theirs is an eternal torment.
   (Qur'an 5:37)

As for the fearful, the unbelieving, the polluted,
the murderous, the decadent, the magicians,
the idolaters, and all who speak falsely,
their place will be in the fiery lake of sulfur.
   (Revelation 21:8)

Disbelievers shall have the punishment of Hell.
O Believers, when you face the disbeliever in battle
do not retreat, for those who retreat—
unless they do so as a tactic to secure victory—
shall surely merit the anger of God.
And their refuge shall be Hell.
   (Qur'an 8:15–16)

I shall terrify the hearts of disbelievers.
So cut off their heads, and slice off their fingertips,
for they are opposed to God and God's messenger,
and whoever opposes God and God's messenger—
surely God is severe in punishment.

    (Qur'an 8:12–13)

Fight the disbelievers
and God will punish them through your hands
and disgrace them,
and God will grant you victory over them
and in so doing strengthen the belief of believers.

    (Qur'an 9:14)

On the Day of Resurrection
we shall gather the unbelievers,
and render them blind, dumb, and deaf,
and their refuge will be Hell.
And when the Fires cool
We shall rekindle them hotter still.
That is their punishment for disbelieving in Our Revelations.

    (Qur'an 17:97–98)

Just as weeds are gathered and set ablaze,
so at the end times the Son of Man
will unleash his angels to rake his kingdom
free of sin and evildoers.
And these will be tossed into a fiery furnace,
weeping and grinding their teeth in agony.

    (Matthew 13:40–42)

For the disbelievers
we have prepared an inescapable Hell.
If they beg for relief,
they shall be showered with water
as hot as molten lead,
an evil drink
burning their faces,
scorching their insides—
how terrible is this resting place!
　　(Qur'an 18:29)

As for disbelievers,
clothes of flame shall be sewn for them,
and their heads soaked in boiling liquid so hot
as to melt their skin and organs,
and they shall be impaled on iron rods.
And should they try to escape their suffering
they are forced back and told,
"Taste the punishment of burning!"
　　(Qur'an 22:19–22)

And he will say to those on his left,
"Cursed ones! Get away from me
and into the eternal fire prepared for Satan and his angels."
　　(Matthew 25:41)

[Jesus speaking to his Jewish opponents:]
You snakes! You vipers!
For you there is no escape from hell.
You are responsible for all the blood
of the righteous shed on earth.
　　(Matthew 23:33, 23:35)

[Jesus speaking to his Jewish opponents:]
You are the Devil's children,
and choose to do the Devil's work.
   (John 8:44)

If a father sells his daughter into bondage,
she shall not go free as male servants go free.
   (Exodus 21:7)

Women should maintain silence in church.
They are not permitted to speak,
and should remain subservient, according to the law.
If they are curious about something,
let them inquire of their husbands at home,
for it is dishonorable for a woman to speak in church.
   (1 Corinthians 14:34–35)

A woman should learn in silence
and complete subservience.
I do not allow women to teach
or to assume authority over men;
they must remain silent.
   (1 Timothy 2:11–12)

Man was not created for woman,
but woman was created for man.
   (1 Corinthians 11:8)

The Eight Points of Agreement

In 1984 Father Thomas Keating invited a small group of contemplatives from eight different religious traditions—Buddhist, Hindu, Jewish, Islamic, Native American, Russian Orthodox, Protestant, and Roman Catholic—to gather at St. Benedict's Monastery in Snowmass, Colorado, to engage in what he called "a big experiment."[1]

The experiment was to see what would happen when meditators from different traditions meditated together and shared the spiritual insights they gleaned from their meditation. Within a few days it became clear to the attendees that while their religious vocabularies were different, their experiences were not. As one attendee put it:

> I enter into meditation as a slice of American cheese: thick and solid;
> my egoic self intact and feeling apart from both God and creation.
> I return from meditation as a slice of Swiss cheese: thin and filled
> with holes. I know myself and all others to be a part of God. Indeed,
> there is no other at all, only the One, the Whole, the Ultimate
> Reality I am calling God. And with this sense of wholeness comes a
> sense of holiness, a sense of love from and for all beings.

While each of the attendees had his or her own way of saying this, all had shared similar experiences.

During the first few years of the Snowmass Conference, a series of agreements arose among the attendees. Father Thomas compiled the first eight and brought them to the group for consideration. With lots of conversation and some editing, the Snowmass Conference Eight Points of Agreement came into being. We include them here as a way of sharing a contemporary expression of perennial wisdom arising not from ancient texts but from the lived experience of contemporary mystics—women and men who, while coming from specific traditions, dare to step beyond them to see what is on its own terms.

The Eight Points of Agreement

1. The world religions bear witness to the experience of Ultimate Reality, to which they give various names.
2. Ultimate Reality cannot be limited by any name or concept.
3. Ultimate Reality is the ground of infinite potentiality and actualization.
4. Faith is opening, accepting, and responding to Ultimate Reality. Faith in this sense precedes every belief system.
5. The potential for human wholeness—or, in other frames of reference, enlightenment, salvation, transcendence, transformation, blessedness—is present in every human being.
6. Ultimate Reality may be experienced not only through religious practices but also through nature, art, human relationships, and service to others.
7. As long as the human condition is experienced as separate from Ultimate Reality, it is subject to ignorance and illusion, weakness and suffering.
8. Disciplined practice is essential to the spiritual life; yet spiritual attainment is not the result of one's own efforts, but the result of the experience of oneness with Ultimate Reality.[2]

Of the eight points, it is the fourth that adds the most to our understanding of perennial wisdom. Faith here is not defined as religion but rather as an "opening, accepting, and responding to Ultimate Reality" that "precedes," and I would add transcends, "every belief system." As I recall one member of the original Snowmass Conference saying:

> Belief narrows my capacity to see what is by insisting that I see only what the belief wants me to see. My belief tells me in advance what I will see, and denies the validity of my seeing if what I see is something other than what the belief wants me to see. This is why Jews, if you'll pardon the reference, cannot see the truth of Christ or Krishna, and why Buddhists cannot see the eternality of Atman and Brahma, and why Muslims cannot accept Bahá'u'lláh as a prophet

and Baha'i as a legitimate religion. It isn't that these rejected views are false, only that they are invisible to those whose beliefs deny them a priori. Faith on the other hand is the capacity to see without the blinders of belief.

Perennial wisdom carries its own beliefs:

- All beings are manifestations of the singular *being*—Ultimate Reality.
- Every human has the innate capacity to know Ultimate Reality outwardly as the Self and inwardly as the Eternal I.
- Knowing Ultimately Reality as Self and the Eternal I gives rise to a global ethic of justice and compassion for all beings.
- The highest purpose of humankind is to know, embody, and live from this truth.

And these beliefs, too, limit what can be seen. Thus even as you seek to awaken to the truth of perennial wisdom, do not close yourself off to an even greater truth: the Tao that cannot be named.

Universal Declaration
of Human Rights

The Universal Declaration of Human Rights was adopted by the United Nations on December 10, 1948, in Paris.[1] The intent of the declaration was to clearly articulate the rights of human beings "without distinction as to race, sex, language, or religion," as the United Nations Charter puts it. The UN commissioned the declaration in 1946, and a group of eighteen representatives of various nationalities and political persuasions was chosen to draft it. Eleanor Roosevelt chaired the committee, and the principal author of the text was John Peters Humphrey, a Canadian legal scholar and human rights activist.

The vote to adopt the declaration was not unanimous. While no nation voted against it and forty-eight nations voted for it, many nations abstained. Those that did so are not surprising. The Soviet Union and Soviet bloc nations were not eager to have their totalitarian regimes challenged by the document, especially its provision that people had the right to leave a nation if they so choose. South Africa abstained in order to protect its system of apartheid. The Kingdom of Saudi Arabia abstained, claiming that the declaration violated sharia, Islamic law, especially Articles 16 and 18: the first insists that marriage cannot be restricted by race, nationality, or religion and can only be entered into with the freely given consent of those about to be married; the second guarantees people the right to change their religion or beliefs. Pakistan, on the other hand, supported the declaration and argued against the Saudi position.

Criticism of the Universal Declaration of Human Rights continues to this day. Current arguments against the declaration claim that it is an act of Western imperialism: imposing liberal, democratic social and political ideals on the rest of the world. But if it is true that the declaration reflects the values of the liberal, democratic West, it is also true that it reflects the values of perennial wisdom, which predate liberal and democratic ideas by millennia.

We include the Universal Declaration of Human Rights in *The World Wisdom Bible* as a modern political expression of those values.

Preamble

Whereas recognition of the inherent dignity and of the equal and inalienable rights of all members of the human family is the foundation of freedom, justice and peace in the world,

Whereas disregard and contempt for human rights have resulted in barbarous acts which have outraged the conscience of mankind, and the advent of a world in which human beings shall enjoy freedom of speech and belief and freedom from fear and want has been proclaimed as the highest aspiration of the common people,

Whereas it is essential, if man is not to be compelled to have recourse, as a last resort, to rebellion against tyranny and oppression, that human rights should be protected by the rule of law,

Whereas it is essential to promote the development of friendly relations between nations,

Whereas the peoples of the United Nations have in the Charter reaffirmed their faith in fundamental human rights, in the dignity and worth of the human person and in the equal rights of men and women and have determined to promote social progress and better standards of life in larger freedom,

Whereas Member States have pledged themselves to achieve, in cooperation with the United Nations, the promotion of universal respect for and observance of human rights and fundamental freedoms,

Whereas a common understanding of these rights and freedoms is of the greatest importance for the full realization of this pledge,

Now, therefore, the General Assembly proclaims this Universal Declaration of Human Rights as a common standard of achievement for all peoples and all nations, to the end that every individual and every organ of society, keeping this Declaration constantly in mind, shall strive by teaching and education to promote respect for these rights and freedoms and by progressive measures, national and international, to secure their universal and effective recognition and observance, both among the peoples of Member States themselves and among the peoples of territories under their jurisdiction.

Article I

All human beings are born free and equal in dignity and rights. They are endowed with reason and conscience and should act towards one another in a spirit of brotherhood.

Article 2

Everyone is entitled to all the rights and freedoms set forth in this Declaration, without distinction of any kind, such as race, colour, sex, language, religion, political or other opinion, national or social origin, property, birth or other status. Furthermore, no distinction shall be made on the basis of the political, jurisdictional or international status of the country or territory to which a person belongs, whether it be independent, trust, non-self-governing or under any other limitation of sovereignty.

Article 3

Everyone has the right to life, liberty and security of person.

Article 4

No one shall be held in slavery or servitude; slavery and the slave trade shall be prohibited in all their forms.

Article 5

No one shall be subjected to torture or to cruel, inhuman or degrading treatment or punishment.

Article 6

Everyone has the right to recognition everywhere as a person before the law.

Article 7

All are equal before the law and are entitled without any discrimination to equal protection of the law. All are entitled to equal protection against any discrimination in violation of this Declaration and against any incitement to such discrimination.

Article 8

Everyone has the right to an effective remedy by the competent national tribunals for acts violating the fundamental rights granted him by the constitution or by law.

Article 9

No one shall be subjected to arbitrary arrest, detention or exile.

Article 10

Everyone is entitled in full equality to a fair and public hearing by an independent and impartial tribunal, in the determination of his rights and obligations and of any criminal charge against him.

Article 11

1. Everyone charged with a penal offence has the right to be presumed innocent until proved guilty according to law in a public trial at which he has had all the guarantees necessary for his defense.
2. No one shall be held guilty of any penal offence on account of any act or omission which did not constitute a penal offence, under national or international law, at the time when it was committed. Nor shall a heavier penalty be imposed than the one that was applicable at the time the penal offence was committed.

Article 12

No one shall be subjected to arbitrary interference with his privacy, family, home or correspondence, nor to attacks upon his honour and reputation. Everyone has the right to the protection of the law against such interference or attacks.

Article 13

1. Everyone has the right to freedom of movement and residence within the borders of each State.
2. Everyone has the right to leave any country, including his own, and to return to his country.

Article 14

1. Everyone has the right to seek and to enjoy in other countries asylum from persecution.
2. This right may not be invoked in the case of prosecutions genuinely arising from non-political crimes or from acts contrary to the purposes and principles of the United Nations.

Article 15

1. Everyone has the right to a nationality.
2. No one shall be arbitrarily deprived of his nationality nor denied the right to change his nationality.

Article 16

1. Men and women of full age, without any limitation due to race, nationality or religion, have the right to marry and to found a family. They are entitled to equal rights as to marriage, during marriage and at its dissolution.
2. Marriage shall be entered into only with the free and full consent of the intending spouses.
3. The family is the natural and fundamental group unit of society and is entitled to protection by society and the State.

Article 17

1. Everyone has the right to own property alone as well as in association with others.
2. No one shall be arbitrarily deprived of his property.

Article 18

Everyone has the right to freedom of thought, conscience and religion; this right includes freedom to change his religion or belief, and freedom, either alone or in community with others and in public or private, to manifest his religion or belief in teaching, practice, worship and observance.

Article 19

Everyone has the right to freedom of opinion and expression; this right includes freedom to hold opinions without interference and to seek, receive and impart information and ideas through any media and regardless of frontiers.

Article 20

1. Everyone has the right to freedom of peaceful assembly and association.
2. No one may be compelled to belong to an association.

Article 21

1. Everyone has the right to take part in the government of his country, directly or through freely chosen representatives.
2. Everyone has the right to equal access to public service in his country.
3. The will of the people shall be the basis of the authority of government; this will shall be expressed in periodic and genuine elections which shall be by universal and equal suffrage and shall be held by secret vote or by equivalent free voting procedures.

Article 22

Everyone, as a member of society, has the right to social security and is entitled to realization, through national effort and international co-operation and in accordance with the organization and resources of each State, of the economic, social and cultural rights indispensable for his dignity and the free development of his personality.

Article 23

1. Everyone has the right to work, to free choice of employment, to just and favourable conditions of work and to protection against unemployment.
2. Everyone, without any discrimination, has the right to equal pay for equal work.

3. Everyone who works has the right to just and favourable remuneration ensuring for himself and his family an existence worthy of human dignity, and supplemented, if necessary, by other means of social protection.
4. Everyone has the right to form and to join trade unions for the protection of his interests.

Article 24

Everyone has the right to rest and leisure, including reasonable limitation of working hours and periodic holidays with pay.

Article 25

1. Everyone has the right to a standard of living adequate for the health and well-being of himself and of his family, including food, clothing, housing and medical care and necessary social services, and the right to security in the event of unemployment, sickness, disability, widowhood, old age or other lack of livelihood in circumstances beyond his control.
2. Motherhood and childhood are entitled to special care and assistance. All children, whether born in or out of wedlock, shall enjoy the same social protection.

Article 26

1. Everyone has the right to education. Education shall be free, at least in the elementary and fundamental stages. Elementary education shall be compulsory. Technical and professional education shall be made generally available and higher education shall be equally accessible to all on the basis of merit.
2. Education shall be directed to the full development of the human personality and to the strengthening of respect for human rights and fundamental freedoms. It shall promote understanding, tolerance and friendship among all nations, racial or religious groups, and shall further the activities of the United Nations for the maintenance of peace.
3. Parents have a prior right to choose the kind of education that shall be given to their children.

Article 27

1. Everyone has the right freely to participate in the cultural life of the community, to enjoy the arts and to share in scientific advancement and its benefits.
2. Everyone has the right to the protection of the moral and material interests resulting from any scientific, literary or artistic production of which he is the author.

Article 28

Everyone is entitled to a social and international order in which the rights and freedoms set forth in this Declaration can be fully realized.

Article 29

1. Everyone has duties to the community in which alone the free and full development of his personality is possible.
2. In the exercise of his rights and freedoms, everyone shall be subject only to such limitations as are determined by law solely for the purpose of securing due recognition and respect for the rights and freedoms of others and of meeting the just requirements of morality, public order and the general welfare in a democratic society.
3. These rights and freedoms may in no case be exercised contrary to the purposes and principles of the United Nations.

Article 30

Nothing in this Declaration may be interpreted as implying for any State, group or person any right to engage in any activity or to perform any act aimed at the destruction of any of the rights and freedoms set forth herein.

Notes

A Note on God

1. Tsai Chih Chung, *Zen Speaks: Shouts of Nothingness*, trans. Brian Bruya (New York: Anchor Books, 1994), 24.

Introduction

1. Stephen Prothero, *God Is Not One: The Eight Rival Religions That Run the World* (New York: HarperOne, 2010), 14.

Chapter Two: The Eternal I

1. Rami Shapiro, *Hasidic Tales: Annotated & Explained* (Woodstock, VT: SkyLight Paths, 2004), 191.
2. Ibid.

Chapter Three: The Self or Mind

1. William Blake, "Augeries of Innocence," in *The Complete Poems*, ed. Alicia Ostriker (New York: Penguin Books USA, 1977), 506.
2. Thich Nhat Hanh, *Being Peace* (Berkeley, CA: Parallax Press, 1987), 51.

Chapter Four: The Nature of Wisdom

1. Albert Einstein, in a letter to Robert S. Marcus, February 12, 1950, www.lettersofnote.com/2011/11/delusion.html.

Chapter Seven: Living Wisely

1. Karen Armstrong, *The Great Transformation: The Beginning of Our Religious Traditions* (New York: Alfred A. Knopf, 2006), 392.

Appendix Two: The Eight Points of Agreement

1. Netanel Miles-Yepez, *The Common Heart: An Experience of Interreligious Dialogue* (New York: Lantern Books, 2006), 1.
2. Ibid., xvii–xviii.

Appendix Three: Universal Declaration of Human Rights

1. Eleanor Roosevelt, *Universal Declaration of Human Rights* (Bedford, MA: Applewood Books, 2001).

Sages Cited, Annotated

Prepared by Aaron Shapiro

Anthony: c. 251–356 CE; also known as Saint Anthony and the Father of All Monks, Abba Anthony was an early Christian ascetic renowned for his sojourn into the Eastern Desert of Egypt. The biography of Anthony's life written by Athanasius helped to spread Christian monasticism. Accounts of Anthony's temptation in the desert also had a profound impact on Western art and literature.

Benjamin: 590–691 CE; thirty-eighth pope of the Coptic Church from 622 until his death in 691 CE. Abba Benjamin is notable for maintaining the unity of the church through three successive eras of political and social upheaval in the Eastern Mediterranean: the Persian occupation (623–638 CE), the return of Byzantine rule (628–640 CE), and the Arab conquest (640 CE). Little is known of Benjamin's early years as pope, but his pontificate was essential to the survival of Egyptian Orthodox Christianity—particularly due to Benjamin's resistance to the imposition of a Chalcedonian pontiff under Byzantine rule, as well as his meeting with the Arab commander 'Amr ibn al-'As, a meeting that secured the restoration of Coptic rights when Persia fell under the control of Islam.

Berekiah: A third-century rabbi known for his commentary on non-legal Jewish texts.

Buddha: See **Gautama, Siddhartha (Buddha).**

Cassian, John: 360–435 CE; known also as John the Ascetic and John Cassian the Roman, he was a Christian theologian and mystic whose writings were pivotal in encouraging the spread of Christian monasticism. Unlike Saint Augustine, who imagines salvation as a function solely of grace, Cassian teaches that salvation—though accompanied and enabled by grace—must also contain a component of free will and involves as well a kind of rehabilitation in grace of the faculty of free choice.

Chaim of Volozhin: 1749–1821 CE; an Orthodox rabbi, Talmudist, and ethicist, Reb Chaim was a prominent student of the Vilna Gaon and founded the Volozhin Yeshiva in 1803. He is the author of the influential kabbalistic text *Nefesh HaChayim* (The Living Soul) as well as of *Ruach Chayim* (Spirit of Life), a commentary on *Pirke Avot*.

Chuang-tzu: Fourth century BCE; Chinese Taoist philosopher. Traditionally, Chuang-tzu, also known as Chuang Chou, is identified as the author of the book that bears his name, the Chuang-tzu, also called *True Classic of Southern (Cultural) Flourescence*. However, the historicity of Chuang-tzu's authorship is debated. Nevertheless, the book is a classic of Taoist philosophy, providing a skeptical, sometimes caustic, and even anarcho-individualistic philosophy quite at odds with the socially minded and duty-bound Confucianism dominant in China at the time.

Confucius: 551–479 BCE; according to Chinese tradition, Confucius was the politician, teacher, and thinker who authored the Analects and founded the *Ru* school of Chinese philosophy. His work forms the foundation of ancient Chinese thought regarding the nature and comportment of the ideal human being, as well as the functioning of ideal political and social systems.

Cordovero, Moshe: 1522–1570 CE; a major early kabbalist and mystic of the sixteenth century and author of *Sefer Elimah*. He was responsible for organizing the widely varied writings of the kabbalists into an integrated, unified system of thought. Cordoverian Kabbalah was later subsumed into Lurianic Kabbalah, and Cordovero's writings are still studied side by side with those of Isaac Luria.

Eliezer: A rabbi of the Talmudic period (70 BC–500 CE) mentioned in *Avot de Rabbi Nathan*; almost nothing is known of Reb Eliezer other than his name.

Evagrios the Solitary: 345–399 CE; also known as Evagrius I, a Christian ascetic monk and a highly influential theologian of the fourth-century church. He is, in fact, one of the first to begin collecting and organizing the aphorisms and apothegms of the monks that would be known as the sayings of the Desert Fathers and Mothers. His own teaching involved a systematic categorization of the varied modes of temptation, as well as discourses on *apatheia*, a state of being without passion.

Gautama, Siddhartha (Buddha): c. 563–483 BCE; a sage of the Shakya republic in India and the founder of Buddhism. Siddhartha's teachings were entirely oral, and they survived in that form, as part of the Buddhist oral tradition, for many centuries before being first written down about four hundred years after the Buddha's death. Key among the tenets of Buddhism are the Four Noble Truths: (1) suffering, or dissatisfaction, is bound up naturally with life's fundamental impermanence; (2) the true cause of suffering is desire, which surfaces in three ways—as craving for sensual pleasures, craving for identity, and craving for annihilation; (3) suffering can be overcome; and (4) the way to overcome it is through an Eightfold Path, consisting of right understanding, right thought, right speech, right action, right livelihood, right effort, right mindfulness, and right concentration.

Gregory of Sinai: c. 1268–1346 CE; a strict ascetic and practitioner of *hesychasm*, Gregory is a saint of the Eastern Orthodox Church. He is perhaps best known for his writings: 15 texts of the *Philokalia* about the inner life called "On Stillness" and an additional 137 texts on living the commandments.

Gregory Palamas: 1296–1359 CE; a Greek monk, archbishop of Thessoliniki, and a saint of the Eastern Orthodox Church. He is well known for his writings defending the practice of *hesychasm*, focusing the mind in a ceaseless act of contemplative prayer designed to bring about an experiential knowledge of God as uncreated light.

Habakkuk: A prophet of the Hebrew Bible, active around the late seventh and early sixth centuries BCE; traditional author of the book of Habakkuk, the eighth of the twelve books of the minor prophets. The book is particularly notable for its willingness to call God to account for inaction in the face of human suffering.

Hesychios the Priest: Eighth-century ascetic whose writings are included in the text of the *Philokalia*, the primary treatise on Christian contemplative prayer. Saint Hesychios is the author of the section entitled "On Watchfulness and Holiness," in which he teaches the contemplative practitioner the process of quieting the heart.

Hiakajo Roshi: Zen master famous for seeing everyday reality as the truth of Zen, and teaching Zen as the radical acceptance of ordinary experience without hesitation or reservation.

Hierax: One of the Desert Fathers, Abba Hierax was a Christian ascetic who lived at Leontoplis in Egypt during the third century CE. He wrote biblical commentaries in both Greek and Coptic and stressed the importance of celibacy to salvation.

Hildegard of Bingen: 1098–1179 CE; known as the Sibyl of the Rhine, Hildegard was a German Benedictine abbess of great accomplishment. She was also a visionary Christian mystic and, having received the approval of the pope, recorded her visions in three major works: *Scivias* (Know the Ways), *Liber Vitae Meritorum* (Book of Life's Merits), and *Liber Divinorum Operum* (Book of Divine Works).

Horowitz, Aharon HaLevi: 1766–1829 CE; Polish Talmudic scholar and kabbalist. HaLevi was the founder of the now-defunct branch of Staroselye Hasidism, created in 1812 following a disagreement between HaLevi and Rabbi Dov Ber over the rightful successor to Reb Schneur Zalman, the first rabbi of the Chabad Hasidic movement. HaLevi's major work, *Sha'arei Avodah* (The Gates of Worship), focuses on the unity of God, the union of souls, the law, and repentance. He is also the author of a work of Torah commentary, *Avodat HaLevi*.

Hosea: Eighth century BCE; Hebrew prophet operating in Northern Israel and traditional author of the biblical book of Hosea, which critiques the resurgence of idolatry within the Northern Kingdom and urges a national repentance.

Hsin Hsin Ming, Third Chinese Patriarch of Zen: Very little is known about Hsin Hsin Ming prior to his legendary meeting with Hui-k'o, the Second Chinese Patriarch of Zen in 551 CE. It was Hui-k'o who, impressed with Hsin Hsin's potential, taught him the dharma. However, not long afterward, persecution against Buddhists in China forced Hsin Hsin into hiding. In 592 CE, he passed his knowledge to the Fourth Chinese Patriarch of Zen, Tao Hsin. He died in 606 CE.

Ibn Ezra, Abraham: 1089–c.1167 CE; a widely traveled, prolific, and distinguished Jewish philosopher of the Middle Ages. Ibn Ezra wrote extensive Torah commentaries, poetry, and secular works in philosophy, astronomy, mathematics, and grammar. His rationalist bent, brought to bear in his commentaries, in some ways lays the groundwork for the documentary hypothesis, by which the Torah is understood to have been compiled from multiple sources written at different times.

Isaac, Priest of the Cells: One of the Desert Fathers, Abba Isaac was an anchorite in Nitria around the third or fourth century CE. He was known for his embrace of extreme poverty and for his highly emotional style of prayer. He was eventually exiled for suspected Origenism.

Isaiah: Eighth century BCE; biblical prophet and presumed author of the book of Isaiah. Isaiah was both witness to and participant in one of the most turbulent periods in the history of Judea, a period marked by Assyrian expansionism and radical Judean political reform under Hezekiah. His prophecies emphasize a progressive vision of history, in which the suffering of the present will eventually be redeemed in an era of universal peace, justice, and prosperity. It is from Isaiah that Judaism takes its conception of its role in the development of world history: the Jews, according to Isaiah, are to be a "light unto the nations," serving as moral and spiritual guides to universal redemption.

Isaiah the Solitary: A monk living in Scetis around 370 CE, Isaiah relocated to Palestine to live as a hermit around 431 CE; he died near Gaza in 491 CE. Isaiah is best known for his contribution to the *Philokalia*: twenty-seven texts on protecting the mind from demonic influence.

James: First century CE; Christian martyr, also known as James the Just, James the Less, and James, son of Alphaeus. James is identified in various Gospels as a brother of Jesus, though whether this is meant biologically or metaphorically is debatable. James worked with Peter as a leader of the church in Jerusalem and became its principal authority when Peter was forced to flee by Herod. He is the author of the Apostolic Decree and the Epistle of James.

Jeremiah: Seventh and sixth centuries BCE; the second of the major canonical Jewish prophets, traditionally thought to have authored the book of
Jeremiah, 1 Kings, 2 Kings, and the book of Lamentations. Jeremiah's ministry spans the period preceding and following the Babylonian exile and
the destruction of the First Temple in Jerusalem. Jeremiah's exhortations
focused primarily on denouncing idolatry, corruption in the priesthood,
and false prophecy.

John the Dwarf: c. 339–c. 405 CE; one of the Desert Fathers and a disciple
of Saint Pambo. John was renowned for his obedience, and legend has it
that Saint Pambo once gave John a dry piece of wood and ordered him to
water it. John continued watering the plank for three years, porting water
from the nearest source, twelve miles away. At the end of that time, the
plank sprouted and grew into a fruit tree. John founded a monastery on the
spot, where the Tree of Obedience remains to this day.

Jose ben Judah: A Talmudic scholar of the latter second century CE, best
known for his various disputes with Judah the Prince, chief redactor and
editor of the Mishnah.

Joseph of Panephysis: One of the Desert Fathers active in the third or
fourth century. He propounded the view, based on Aristotelian philosophy,
that one's passions have their source in God and thus are to be mastered and
illuminated by faith rather than overcome or annihilated.

Julian of Norwich: A visionary Christian mystic and anchoress of the four-
teenth century. Julian's sixteen visions are recorded in her only known
work, *Revelations of Divine Love*, which comes to us in two forms: the short
text, containing only the visions themselves and Julian's interpretations,
and the long text, which appends her theological commentary.

Krishna: A major figure in Hindu religious texts, he is considered to be the
eighth incarnation of the Lord Vishnu, the supreme deity of Hinduism. The
mythology surrounding Krishna is primarily derived from the *Mahabharata*
as well as from the *Harivamsha* and books 10 and 11 of the *Bhagavata-purana*.
Krishna is sometimes also identified as a historical person, and some religious scholars have argued that he may have been Vasudeva Govinda Krishna
Sharui, a tribal ruler who lived sometime around 3100–3200 BCE.

Lao Tzu: Sixth century BCE; Chinese philosopher traditionally credited with founding philosophic Taoism and authoring the *Tao Te Ching*. Scholars today dispute the historicity of these claims, with some arguing that Lao Tzu lived during the fourth or fifth century BCE during the golden age of Chinese philosophy, a period in which a wide range of philosophical ideas were widely discussed and freely debated. Some scholars, moreover, have argued that Lao Tzu is a historical composite. Regardless, he is a central figure of Taoist philosophy, and his work has been influential to a number of anti-authoritarian movements in Chinese and world history.

Levi Yitzchak of Berditchev: 1740–1810; a leading scholar and chief rabbi of a number of Jewish communities in Poland. Reb Yitzchak became one of the most influential leaders of the early Hasidic movement in Eastern Europe. He is known primarily for his compassion in interpreting the doings of the Jews, and it was widely believed that he might act as a "defense attorney" for the Jewish people, mitigating their judgment by God. His major works include *Kedushas Levi*, a Torah commentary; the popular liturgical song "Dudele"; and a liturgical poem, "The Kaddish of Rebbe Levi Yitzchak."

Lot: Active in or around the third or fourth century CE, Abba Lot was a Coptic monk and disciple of Joseph of Panephysis; Lot's teachings, and particularly his opposition to Origenism, are recorded in *Apophthegmata Patrum* (Sayings of the Desert Fathers).

Macarius: c. 300–391 CE; also known as Saint Macarius the Great and Macarius of Egypt, Abba Macarius was a disciple of Saint Anthony the Great and one of the Desert Fathers; his *Fifty Spiritual Homilies* is a classic early Christian text stressing self-subdual and devotion to God.

Maximos the Confessor: 586–662 CE; Greek Orthodox monk and proponent of Neoplatonist theology, which argues that salvation consists of humankind's spiritual reunion with God. Maximos was also deeply embroiled in the Monothelite controversy, a disagreement over the nature of Christ's will. Monothelism holds that Christ had a singular will, synonymous with the will of God the Father. Maximos opposed the Monothelites, asserting that Christ had both a human and a divine will. His opposition brought him into conflict with the religious authorities of his time and resulted in his being tried and convicted of heresy, though he was later vindicated by the Sixth Ecumenical Council (also called the Third Council of Constantinople).

Micah: Biblical prophet whose prophetic activity spanned the period 737–690 BCE. Micah is best known for prophesying against the corruption of the ruling class and the priesthood in the Kingdom of Judah. He predicts the destruction of Jerusalem but also lays the groundwork for the Jewish messianic vision, imagining a time when Jerusalem will be restored.

Moses (Abba): 330–405 CE; a reformed thief, Abba Moses converted to Christianity while hiding from local authorities among the monks of the ascetic community in Sketes near Alexandria. Following his conversion, Abba Moses became an effective spiritual leader and a proponent of nonviolence.

Muhammad: 570–632 CE; the founder of Islam and the political and military leader who unified Arabia into a single political and socio-religious entity. According to Islamic tradition, Muhammad is the final prophet of Allah (God), and his revelations, recorded in the Qur'an, signify the culmination of the Judeo-Christian prophetic tradition.

Nilus: Very little is known about Abba Nilus other than he is counted as one of the Desert Fathers and lived during the third or fourth century as an ascetic monk in the desert of Egypt. His recorded sayings are few and focus entirely on the nature and method of proper prayer.

Noson, Reb (Nathan Sternhartz): 1780–1844; commonly known as Rabbi Noson, Sternhartz was the chief disciple of Reb Nachman of Breslov, the founder of Breslov Hasidism. He is largely responsible for preserving Reb Nachman's teachings, stories, and conversations as well as for expanding the Breslov movement after his mentor's death.

Paul: First century CE; the apostle Paul, once Saul of Tarsus. Famously converted to Christianity on the road to Damascus after having been an intense opponent, Paul is one of the greatest and most influential figures of early Christianity, responsible for spreading the gospel of Jesus throughout the gentile communities of the Roman Empire. Paul's epistles, of course, are included as a canonical part of the New Testament.

Peter of Damaskos: First century CE; one of the twelve disciples of Jesus, a prominent leader of the first-century Christian movement, and a saint of the Catholic Church, which traditionally considers him to have founded the Holy See in concert with Paul. Peter's life story is told in the canonical Gospels, along with the book of Acts, the Hebrew Gospel, and other writings of the early church.

Poemen: c. 340–450 CE; an Egyptian monk and saint of Eastern Christianity. Abba Poemen (Shepherd) is the most widely quoted of the Desert Fathers and is known for his tolerance and compassion, as well as for his eschewal of religious authority, disinterest in the extremes of asceticism, and emphasis on providing gentle spiritual guidance. Poemen seems to have been forced into the desert life, fleeing the monastery at Scetis when that early center of monasticism was overrun by raiders. It was Abba Poemen and his group who recorded the sayings tradition of desert monasticism in the book called *Apophthegmata Patrum* (Sayings of the Desert Fathers). However, some scholars— noting the sheer number of quotations attributed to Poemen—have argued that his name became a kind of catchall and that some of the sayings attributed to him were in fact the sayings of other, unnamed desert ascetics.

Rufus: One of the Desert Fathers active in the third and fourth centuries; like many of his brethren, Abba Rufus stressed contemplative practices designed to move the practitioner to *hesychia*, a place of inner stillness and quietude from which to experience God's grace.

Sarah (Amma): One of the Desert Mothers living in Egypt, Persia, and Palestine during the fourth and fifth centuries. The sayings tradition of the Desert Mothers is partially recorded in *Apophthegmata Patrum* (Sayings of the Desert Fathers), which contains forty-seven sayings attributed to various *ammas*, or mothers, of the desert monastic communities. Amma Sarah, also referred to as Sarah of the Desert, seems to have had a rather caustic wit and to have stressed purity of heart over the maintenance of social (and gender) norms.

Schneur Zalman of Liady: 1745–1812; founder of Chabad Hasidism, which stresses an intellectual approach to faith as well as an intellectual approach to the interpretation of Talmudic and kabbalistic texts. Indeed, in his commentaries, Reb Zalman sought to assert a rational basis for both Hasidism and Kabbalah.

Sirach, Jesus ben: A Jewish scribe of the early second century BCE; also known as Ben Sira or Joshua. He is the author of the apocryphal Wisdom of Jesus ben Sirach, included in the Septuagint, the Greek translation of the Hebrew Bible. Though little is known of his life, it is thought that he authored the work while living in Alexandria sometime between 180 and 175 BCE.

Stithatos, Nikitas: 1005–1090; a Christian mystic and saint of the Eastern Orthodox Church. Stithatos is famed as the author *The Life of Symeon*, a biography of his friend and teacher Symeon the Theologian. He is also noted for having defended Symeon's teaching of the *hesychast* prayer and for writing a number of treatises on Gnostic theology now collected in the *Philokalia*. Stithatos's most important works in this regard are "On the Soul," "On Paradise," and "On the Hierarchy."

Syncletica of Alexandria: A fourth-century Christian ascetic and one of the Desert Mothers. Amma Syncletica and her sister, though born to a respected family, divested themselves of their material wealth and moved into the desert to live as monastics. Amma Syncletica's teachings focus on living a life of discernment, making choices based on humility, reflection, and prayer so as to live better in harmony with the Divine.

Thalassios the Libyan: A friend of Maximos the Confessor and abbot of a monastery in Libya during the seventh century. Saint Thalassios is the author of "On Love, Self-Control, and Life in Accordance with the Intellect," one of the chapters of *Philokalia*. In his writing, Saint Thalassios emphasizes the unity of the soul with the body along with the importance of love.

Theodora: One of the fourth-century Desert Mothers, an associate of Archbishop Theophilus of Alexandria, and an authority on monastic life. Amma Theodora's teachings emphasize self-discipline, especially of the passions and the pursuit of inner peace.

Theodoros the Great Ascetic: A monk at Sabas near Jerusalem active in the ninth century who later became bishop of Edessa in Syria. The facts of his life, especially as recorded by Basil of Emesa, are disputed, as is his authorship of parts of the *Philokalia*. While one of the works with which he is credited, *A Century of Spiritual Texts*, is likely his own, his authorship of the second, *Theoretikon*, is questioned on the basis of its presumed date of composition.

Theognostos II: Active during the fourth century, nothing is known about Theognostos II other than his purported authorship of a section of the *Philokalia* entitled "On the Practice of the Virtues." Theognostos's writings stress asceticism and contemplation along with unceasing desire (expressed in prayer) as means to the development of spiritual knowledge.

Yose ben Yoezer: Known for his asceticism and piety, Rabbi Yose ben Yoezer was a disciple of Antigonos of Sokho and, together with Yose ben Yochanan, were the two leading sages (*zuggot*, couples) of the Maccabean period (164–63 BCE).

Zechariah: One of the twelve minor Hebrew prophets, active during the period 520–518 BCE. The primary emphasis of Zechariah's writings is on messianic fulfillment.

Primary Sources, Annotated

Prepared by Aaron Shapiro

Acts: The fifth book of the New Testament and the companion to the Gospel according to Luke. Acts narrates the events surrounding the founding of the Christian church and the spread of Christianity through the Roman Empire. Though its author is unknown, it is traditionally attributed to Luke and is dated to around 80–90 CE.

Acts of Peter: Composed in Greek during the second half of the second century but surviving only in Latin translations, the Acts of Peter is among the oldest apocryphal texts dealing with the apostles.

Analects, the: A collection of the sayings of Confucius, compiled by his students between 471 and 221 BCE, and achieving its complete form by the time of the early Han Dynasty (206–220 CE). The Analects is considered one of the principal books of ancient Chinese philosophy. It focuses primarily on the cultivation of moral virtue, beginning with a focus on the individual and then extending that focus to one's family, one's community, and the state.

Apophthegmata Patrum: Strictly translated as "Sayings of the Desert Fathers" though sayings of the Desert Mothers are included as well; the collective wisdom of Christian ascetics who lived primarily in the Egyptian wilderness in the third to sixth centuries CE. These teachings originally circulated orally in Coptic, the language spoken by the Desert Mothers and Fathers, and were collected and written down beginning in the fourth century CE.

Avot de Rabbi Nathan: The first of the minor tractates of the Talmud; compiled sometime during the period 700–900 CE, the text comprises an exposition of *Pirke Avot* and contains many passages and incidents that are entirely unique within the early Rabbinic tradition.

Babylonian Talmud: From the Hebrew root word *l-m-d*, "to teach," the Talmud is an anthology of Rabbinic teaching that, along with the Hebrew Bible, forms the bedrock of Judaism. The Talmud consists of two parts: the Mishnah, the earliest collection of Rabbinic teaching, compiled around 200 CE, and the Gemara, a commentary on the Mishnah, the Hebrew Bible, and other subjects pertinent to Jewish life, compiled around 500 CE. More a library of diverse opinions about Judaism than a cohesive presentation of Judaism, the Talmud deals with Jewish law, ethics, customs, folklore, history, theology, and philosophy.

Bhagavad Gita: A seven-hundred-verse scripture contained in the Hindu epic *Mahabharata*. Set on the battlefield at the start of the Kurukshetra War, the Gita tells the story of Arjuna, a Pendavra prince, who, faced with the prospect of fighting a civil war against his own relatives, teachers, and friends, is filled with doubt. He turns to his charioteer, secretly the Lord Krishna, who responds to his moral confusion by elaborating on concepts of duty and philosophy. The text has been read as an allegory for the moral struggle of each individual, and it offers a prescription of knowledge, devotion, and desireless action as the way to achieve personal salvation.

Book of Divine Works: The last volume of the visionary theological writings of Hildegard of Bingen, a German Benedictine abbess and Christian mystic who lived and wrote during the Middle Ages (1098–1179 CE). The book offers an extended meditation on the theological, salvific, and historical implications of John's "In the beginning was the Word...." It is divided into ten visions and three sections: the first investigating the nature of God's work in the world as well as the relationship between humankind and creation (which Hildegard sees as metonymic, with humanity as part to the universe's whole), the second ruminating on the first six days of creation, and the third describing the historical unfolding of humanity's salvation by God.

Brihadaranyaka Upanishad: One of the ten principal Upanishads and a key text in Hindu theology. Written in Sanskrit, most of the text is thought to have been composed around 700 BCE, though some sections are dated later. The Brihadaranyaka Upanishad offers an extensive exposition of the relationship between Atman and Brahma (read as: the individual and God, or self and Self, soul and Soul), arguing in essence that the two are inextricably One.

Chandogya Upanishad: One of the ten principal Upanishads—the ten major Hindu scriptures—the Chandogya Upanishad presents a system of meditative practice designed to lead the reader to transcend the divisive illusions of egoic self-consciousness and its experience of temporal reality (the "wheel" of birth, life, death), and thus to move beyond suffering by embracing the knowledge of ultimate Self and regaining a connection to the original Source of Being.

Chuang-tzu: Scholars debate its authorship, but Chinese tradition has it that this text records the teachings and writings of Chuang-tzu, a highly influential sage of the fourth century BCE, along with the writings and teachings of his followers and related philosophers. An important precursor to the development of Chinese Zen Buddhism, the text presents a frequently skeptical philosophy, posing essential questions on the nature of self and knowledge. In addition, the text includes meditations on what might be termed an individualist form of anarchism, as well as satirical pieces targeted at contemporaneous schools of philosophy, such as Confucianism.

1 Corinthians: Also known as the First Letter to the Corinthians, this New Testament epistle was written in Ephesus during Paul's sojourn there in the period 53–57 CE. The text responds to Paul's concern over divisions within the church he founded at Corinth and by the immorality wrought by the continued influence of paganism within that church. In his letter, Paul addresses a range of difficulties and offers various fixes, touching as he does so on issues such as the resolution of personal disputes, sexual purity, marriage, Christian liberty, proper worship, and the doctrine of resurrection.

Deuteronomy: The fifth book of the Hebrew Bible, Deuteronomy consists of three sermons delivered by Moses near the end of his life, as the Jews are about to enter into Canaan, the Promised Land. The first sermon recapitulates the narrative of the Jews wandering in the desert after the Exodus; the second reasserts the necessity of the Jews' allegiance to God and to God's law, an allegiance upon which their possession of the Promised Land depends; the third, however, offers the promise that should the Jews prove unfaithful and the land be lost, they may restore themselves through repentance. Though tradition accepts Moses's authorship, modern scholarship suggests that the book's origins lie in the period following Assyria's destruction of the Northern Kingdom of Israel, when the Southern King-dom (Judah) adapted Israeli traditions to a program of political and religious reform. The final form of the text, meanwhile, only emerged in the sixth century BCE, after the Jews' return to Judah from Babylonian captivity.

Dhammapada: Roughly translated as "the path of truth, harmony, and righ-teousness," the Dhammapada consists of 423 verses recording various sayings of the Buddha. The sayings were set down by the Buddha's disciples following his death and are organized into twenty-six chapters according to theme. By crystallizing the Buddha's teaching in this way, the Dhammapada not only preserved the Buddha's teaching but also made it widely accessible. Today, the Dhammapada is the best known and most commonly read Buddhist scripture.

Dharmakaya Sutra: A Buddhist meditation focused on the idea that in order to discover one's true self, one must know oneself as one is prior to the birth and death of all things.

Diamond Sutra: A key text of Zen Buddhism, the Diamond Sutra takes the form of a conversation between the Buddha and a senior monk in which the Buddha, through the technique of negation, breaks down the monk's preconceived notions about the nature of reality and stresses the notion that all worldly phenomena are illusory and that enlightenment depends upon the recognition of the ultimate emptiness of our concepts of identity, of self, and other.

Doctrine of the Mean: One of the four books of Confucian philosophy, gen-erally attributed to Confucius's grandson Zisi. The title of the text is drawn from a verse in the Analects of Confucius, but where Confucius does not elaborate on the term, Zisi does. The doctrine involves living in harmony with nature and contains three guidelines for right living: self-watchfulness (involving self-education, self-questioning, and self-discipline), leniency (compassion, empathy, and reciprocity), and sincerity (defined as connec-tion between humanity and the Divine).

Ecclesiastes: Part of the Writings (*Ketuvim*) section of the Hebrew Bible, Ecclesiastes is traditionally attributed to King Solomon, though the text is in fact anonymous and was likely written sometime near the end of the third century BCE. The book takes the form of an autobiography, detailing the main character's investigations into the meaning of life and the best way of living. The book argues that the actions of humanity are "vain" or "empty" and that human wisdom may have no bearing on eternal truth. It concludes by saying that because both intellectual and personal ambition are rendered absurd by the inevitability and universality of death, one should forgo them and simply enjoy the small pleasures of daily life.

Exodus: The second book of the Hebrew Bible, which relates the story of the Jews' liberation from Egyptian slavery. Led by their prophet, Moses, the Jews journey through the desert to Mount Sinai, where they enter into a covenant with God, who gives them their laws and promises them the land of Canaan in return for their faithfulness. Jewish tradition attributes the authorship of Exodus to Moses; modern scholars, however, see the book as a product of the Babylonian exile.

Galatians: Also known as the Letter to the Galatians. It is the ninth book of the New Testament and another of Paul's epistles, written to the Christian communities of Galatia in response to Paul's concerns about the controversy surrounding the necessity of gentile Christians' adherence to Mosaic Law. Paul takes the position, now fundamental to Christian theology, that Galatian gentiles do not need to follow Mosaic Law and in particular do not need to practice circumcision, as the law of Moses is best understood as a temporary measure rendered obsolete by the embodied revelation of the divine Logos in/as Jesus Christ. Thus Paul's letter lays the groundwork for supersessionism, the Christian theological view positing that the New Covenant (that is, the covenant sealed by the crucifixion of Jesus) has replaced the Mosaic Covenant and that Christians have succeeded Jews as the chosen people of God.

Genesis: The first book of the Hebrew Bible, Genesis relates the story of God's creation of the world and humanity, as well as the story of the formation of the people of Israel. The basic narrative moves from the initial act of creation through the Fall of Man in the Garden of Eden and on to the story of the Flood, in which God, horrified at the wickedness of humankind, attempts to unmake the world, saving only Noah and his family. The post-Flood narrative tracks the story of the Patriarchs, as Abraham is told by God to leave his home and go to Canaan. There Abraham makes a covenant with God, who promises the land to Abraham and his descendants, who live there for three generations, from Abraham to Isaac to Jacob. Following another encounter with God, Jacob's name is changed to Israel, and through the agency of Jacob's son Joseph, the entire people is moved into Egypt, where they (briefly) prosper. Like the book of Exodus (see above), the authorship of Genesis is attributed to Moses, though scholars date the redaction of the book to around the sixth century BCE.

Gospel of Eve: A lost Gnostic book of the New Testament Apocrypha; the only surviving elements of the text appear as quotations in the *Panarion* of Epiphanius.

Gospel of Philip: A noncanonical Gnostic gospel of the Nag Hammadi library, the Gospel of Philip dates to the third century CE and takes the form of an anthology of Gnostic teachings presented without narrative context. The primary theme of the text seems to be sacrament, but the text is best known for being the source of the theory that Mary Magdalene was, in fact, Jesus's wife or partner.

Gospel of Thomas: A noncanonical gospel discovered among the codices of the Nag Hammadi library, the Gospel of Thomas records 116 sayings of Jesus, sometimes embedded in brief parables or dialogues. Some scholars have seen the Gospel of Thomas as a record of the early Christian oral tradition and proof of the existence of the Q Gospel, the theoretical source of the sayings of Jesus that appear, at times word for word, across the canonical Gospels.

Hadith of Bukhari: One of six major collections of hadith (reports of the Prophet Muhammad's words, deeds, and actions) compiled by the Persian Muslim scholar Muhammad al-Bukhari. The text is central to Sunni Islam and is often considered second in importance only to the Qur'an.

Hadith of Gabriel: Collected sayings of the Prophet Muhammad taken from the texts of his recorded speeches and intended as an introductory guide to Islamic belief and practice, touching on issues of purification, prayer, mourning, pilgrimage, jihad, and compassion, among other spiritual topics. The Hadith of Gabriel is the principal Hadith of Sunni Islam, and contains many of the religion's major precepts, including the Five Pillars of Islam, the Six Articles of Faith, and the concept of *Ihsan*, the perfection or excellence of one's faith as expressed in prayer and compassionate action.

Institutes and Conferences: A massive volume that provides an early blueprint for Christian monasticism; written by John Cassian (c. 350–c. 435 CE), one of the Christian monastics known today as the Desert Fathers. A series of dialogues with leading Egyptian spiritual masters, the text focuses on integrating the principle of denial of self into one's daily life.

Isha Upanishad: One of the ten principal Upanishads and a key scripture of Vedanta Hinduism, this brief text is concerned primarily with exhorting one to pursue knowledge of Atman, the Self that is Absolute Reality, so as to liberate oneself from sorrow and suffering.

James: Also known as the Letter of James, it is one of the twenty-two epistles of the New Testament, likely written in the first or second century and traditionally attributed to James the Just. Considered to be an example of Christian wisdom literature, the letter is celebrated for its appeals to care for the poor, to resist oppression without resorting to violence, and to reject worldly knowledge in favor of heavenly understanding while pursuing a course of peacemaking, righteousness, and justice.

Jerusalem Talmud: A collection of Rabbinic commentaries on the Mishnah, or Jewish oral tradition. Like the Babylonian Talmud, the Jerusalem Talmud contains the textual redaction of the Mishnah completed by Judah the Prince in 200 CE along with the written commentaries, compiled between 340 and 400 CE, of generations of Israeli scholars associated with the rabbinical academies at Tiberias and Caesarea. Though similar to the Babylonian Talmud in many ways, the Jerusalem Talmud is not considered authoritative within the Jewish tradition. The Babylonian Talmud is preferred, as it contains more and later commentaries and is thus considered to be a more complete collection of available rabbinical opinion.

Joel: The book of Joel is one of twelve minor prophetic books contained in the Hebrew Bible. In it, Joel laments the arrival of a plague of locusts and a severe drought, argues that these are punishments for Israel's failure to uphold God's commandments, and exhorts the Jews to a national repentance.

John: The fourth canonical Gospel of the New Testament, the Gospel according to John provides an account of the life and ministry of Jesus. The text opens with John the Baptist's affirmation of Jesus and closes with Jesus's death, resurrection, and final appearances. John presents a unique vision of Jesus, describing him as the incarnation of Logos, or the Divine Word.

1 John: Also known as the First Letter of John or the First Epistle of John, it was most likely composed between 95 and 110 CE and attributed to John the Evangelist. One of the books of the New Testament, the text responds to concerns about the fracturing of the Christian community and the influence of heterodox teachers, specifically those who claimed that Christ was not embodied and came to earth as spirit only. In doing so, it lays out three essential tests by which one might discern true spiritual teachers: one will know them, that is, by their ethics, by their assertion of Christ's embodiment in the flesh, and by their love.

Katha Upanishad: One of the ten principal Upanishads, often also referred to by the alternate title "Death as Teacher," the Katha Upanishad tells the story of a boy, Nachiketa, who, in a conversation with Yama, the god of death, learns the secret of life. According to Yama, there are two paths in life: one focuses on the pleasures of the senses and the things of this world and leads only to death; the second path focuses on an inward, spiritual journey, whose end is union with the Divine and immortality.

Kena Upanishad: Second in the Hindu canon of 108 Upanishads, the Kena Upanishad is significant for its discussion of Brahma, which asserts that knowledge of Brahma is beyond the reach of empiricism and as such cannot be worshipped because it cannot be objectified. Rather, knowledge of Brahma is a gestalt awakening to and identification with the Source of All.

Kevaddha Sutta: A Buddhist scripture that takes its name from one of its principal characters, the householder Kevaddha. In the scripture's narrative, Kevaddha invites the Buddha into his home and exhorts him to prove his spiritual development by performing a series of miracles. The Buddha refuses, arguing that supernatural powers are an inadequate sign of a person's spiritual development.

Lankavatara Sutra: Central to Chinese, Tibetan, and Japanese Buddhism, especially Ch'an and Zen, the Lankavatara Sutra records a conversation between Buddha and a disciple named Mahamati (Great Wisdom) in which

Buddha reveals that consciousness is the only reality, and that all reality is a manifesting of mind alone.

Leviticus: The third book of the Hebrew Bible. Though traditionally attributed to Moses, Leviticus is thought by scholars to have been developed much later in the history of Israel and to have been completed either late in the period of the Judean monarchy (seventh century BCE) or during the exilic and post-exilic period of the sixth and fifth centuries BCE. In brief, the book provides instructions for living Jewishly and emphasizes ritual, legal, and ethical practices. Broadly, the book explicates the methods of sacrifice, the rules of priesthood, the distinction between purity and uncleanliness, the nature and methods of atonement, and the path of holiness.

Likkutei Torah: The second volume of a set of the Hebrew Bible commentaries written by the first rebbe of Chabad Hasidism, Rabbi Schneur Zalman of Liady. The first volume, entitled *Torah Or*, covers the texts of Genesis and Exodus, while the second covers Leviticus, Numbers, and Deuteronomy. Together, these two volumes are classics of Chabad philosophy and are studied in Chabad communities alongside the weekly Torah portion.

Luke: The third canonical Gospel of the New Testament, the Gospel according to Luke (like John) bears witness to the life of Jesus, tracing his story from birth to ascension. The text emphasizes Jesus's compassion and contains some material—such as the Prodigal Son and Good Samaritan parables—not present in the other Gospels.

Maitri Upanishad: Twenty-fourth in the canon of 108 Upanishads, the Maitri Upanishad explores the universal nature of Atman (Soul/Self), the primacy and necessity of meditation as a religious activity, ego and egoic attachment as the source and cause of human suffering, and the liberation of consciousness into joyful oneness with Brahma. The text also contains a series of appendices touching on a wide range of subjects, which, among other things, expands the earlier consideration of Atman and which warns against false teachers, encouraging one to follow one's own path to truth.

Mulamadhyamakakarika: The best known book by the Buddhist sage Nagarjuna (d. 250 CE) the Mulamadhyamakakarika (Fundamental Verses of the Middle Way) is the central text of the Madhyamaka School of Buddhism that posits the absence of any permanent substance in the universe.

Mark: The second canonical Gospel of the New Testament, the Gospel according to Mark bears witness to Jesus's life and ministry from the time of his baptism through his death and the discovery of his empty tomb. Once considered by scholars to be a summary of the text of Matthew, it is now thought be the earliest of the Gospels. Moreover, while the text is traditionally attributed to Mark the Evangelist, scholars now regard it as being the work of an unknown writer working with multiple sources.

Matthew: The first of the canonical Gospels of the New Testament, the Gospel according to Matthew begins with the baptism of Jesus and moves on to record his ministry, his trial, the crucifixion, the resurrection, and the giving of the Great Commission. Matthew also contains five discourses of Jesus, including the Sermon on the Mount.

Mundaka Upanishad: Couched as a conversation between Shaunaka and Angiras, the Mundaka Upanishad is a mantra Upanishad, written in verse, and designed to teach the knowledge of Brahma (the Godhead). The text divides knowledge into two broad categories: *Apara Vidya* (knowledge of the material world) and *Para Vidya* (knowledge of Eternal Truth). Both are necessary: *Apara Vidya* enables the accomplishments of the sciences and rationality, but it cannot make known the origins of reality or the root cause of being; *Para Vidya* opens the doors of perception to the underlying fabric of creation. The text discusses the path by which one may comprehend *Para Vidya* and includes such injunctions as the renouncement of all action and the practice of yoga for self-realization. Finally, the text discusses the passage of the soul into Brahma and the annihilation of the perspective of the egoic self within the larger cosmic selfhood of God.

Nefesh HaChayim: The major work of the Orthodox rabbi, Talmudist, and ethicist Chaim of Volozhin, a student of the Vilna Gaon and the founder of the Volozhin Yeshiva. *Nefesh HaChayim* (The Living Soul) comments on a range of subjects, including the nature of the Divine, the nature of the soul, and the nature of the world to come, as well as the efficacy of prayer and *mitzvot* (spiritual disciplines) and the importance of Torah.

Nipata Sutta: Among the earliest if not the earliest collection of teachings by the Buddha, the sutta (sutra) is thought to describe the original practices of the first Buddhists.

Philippians: Also known as the Letter to the Philippians, this is the eleventh book of the New Testament, attributed to Paul of Tarsus and dated around 62 CE. Addressed to the Christian community in Philippi, the first Christian community in Europe, which Paul himself established, the letter is written at a moment when Paul has been imprisoned for preaching the Gospel. In it, Paul focuses much of his writing on exhorting the community to humility, harmony, and unity, though the text also includes a polemic against those Paul terms Judaizers, that is, anyone who would impose on gentile Christians the burdens of Mosaic Law.

Philokalia: An anthology of texts written between the fourth and fifteenth centuries CE by spiritual masters of the Eastern Orthodox Church and intended as guides for monks. The texts offer instruction on meditative and contemplative practices in the *hesychast* tradition, wherein one focuses inward during prayer, seeking to minimize sensory perception.

Pirke Avot: Also known as Ethics of the Sages, *Pirke Avot* is a collection of the ethical teachings and maxims of the early Rabbinic sages divided into six chapters. It appears in the Talmud within tractate *Avot* and is unique among Talmudic writings in that it is not augmented with commentary by later scholars or sages.

Proverbs: One of the twenty-four books composing the Hebrew Bible, Proverbs appears as the second book in Writings (*Ketuvim*). Traditionally attributed to Solomon but thought to have been compiled long after his time, Proverbs is classified as a work of wisdom literature, in which wisdom is frequently personified and defined by contrast to a "fool" character. Proverbs, like much wisdom literature, is specifically interested in examining the relationship between the mundane and the sublime (or divine).

Psalms: The first book of Writings (*Ketuvim*), the third section of the Hebrew Bible. The book collects a range of liturgical poems more or less divisible into five general types: hymns, which praise God's creation or intervention into history; communal laments, which mourn collective catastrophes;

royal psalms, dedicated to coronations, marriages, and battles; individual laments, which grieve the speaker's individual experience of hardship; and individual thanksgiving psalms, which thank God for the speaker's deliverance from sorrow and suffering.

Qur'an: The central religious text of Islam; within Islamic tradition, the Qur'an is considered to be the record of a series of revelations given to the Prophet Muhammad by the angel Gabriel over a period of twenty-three years, from 609 to 632 CE. Muslims regard the Qur'an as the culmination of an ancient lineage of prophetic revelations beginning with Adam and including Abraham, Moses, David, and Jesus.

Revelations of Divine Love: A fourteenth-century Middle English devotional work by the anchoress Julian of Norwich, detailing sixteen mystical visions and meditations on the theme of the pain of sin obviated by God's universal love and compassion.

Rig Veda: One of the four canonical scriptures, called the Vedas, at the heart of Hinduism. The Rig Veda is one of the oldest extant texts in an Indo-European language and is dated to between 1700 and 1100 BCE. The text is organized into ten mandalas (books) containing multiple accounts of the origin of the world, hymns to the gods as well as hymns for life events such as marriage and death, and a wide range of prayers.

Romans: Also known as the Letter to the Romans, this is the longest of Paul's epistles and the fullest explication of his theology. Key to the letter is Paul's universalism, that is, his assurance that salvation is open to all believers, as well as his insistence that salvation arises from faith rather than from works. The letter is also notable in laying out Paul's sense that belief in Christ mitigated the requirements of Mosaic Law and resulted in a radical renewal of the mind that freed believers from bondage to sin and opened them to a transformative love that in itself constituted the fulfillment of the law.

Secret Book of John: Part of the collection of works uncovered in Nag Hammadi in 1945, the Secret Book of John, also known as the Apocryphon of John, is a key text in the tradition of Gnostic Christianity, outlining that tradition's cosmology. Couched in a framing tale, wherein the resurrected Jesus returns to relate a secret revelation to the apostle John, the narrative recounts an alternate history of the creation of the universe and of humankind, one that provocatively revises and even reverses many of the set pieces in the opening chapters of Genesis.

Sefer Elimah: Written in the mid-sixteenth century by Rabbi Moshe Cordovero, a foundational kabbalist thinker, *Sefer Elimah* is one of a number of Cordoverian writings elucidating and systematizing the philosophy of Kabbalah. This particular text deals primarily with the relationship between the Godhead and the *sephirot* (emanations of the divine light).

Sha'arei HaYichud veHaEmunah: Translated as "The Gates of Unity and Faith." One of three compilations of the teachings of Rabbi Schneur Zalman of Liady anthologized by Rabbi Aharon HaLevi Horowitz, considered by the now defunct Staroselye branch of Chabad Hasidism to be the true successor to Chabad's founder. This text examines the Hasidic notion of immanence, that is, the idea that God is present within all things.

Shabbat: A tractate of the Mishnah that also appears in both the Babylonian and the Jerusalem Talmuds. The text deals primarily with the laws for proper observance of the Sabbath.

Shi'ur Qomah to Zohar: A kabbalistic midrashic text in the *Heichalot* genre (which records accounts of mystical ascents to heaven for the purposes of enlightenment or illumination), *Shi'ur Qomah* is written in the form of a collection of teachings revealed to the Tannaitic sage Rabbi Yishmael by the angel Metatron. It contains a rather controversially anthropomorphic anatomy of the Divine as well as an exegesis of the Song of Songs.

Sirach: Also known as the Wisdom of Jesus ben Sirach; a work of the second-century scribe Joshua ben Sirach. Originally a Hebrew text, the Wisdom of Jesus ben Sirach was not accepted into the Jewish liturgical canon; it survived in Greek translation as part of the Septuagint, however, and some original Hebrew texts have now been discovered. The book seems to be modeled on Proverbs; it is written in verse and contains a set of maxims dealing with an individual's duty to self, family, society, the state, the poor, and most especially God.

Tao Te Ching: Classic Chinese philosophical text written in the sixth century BCE and attributed to the sage Lao Tzu. The actual authorship and dating of the text are still debated, though some have postulated that parts of the text may date to the fourth century BCE. The Tao Te Ching is essential to philosophical and religious Taoism and has had wide-ranging influence on other schools of thought, including Buddhism. The text is organized into eighty-one short poems and contains a total of five thousand characters. The poems deal with a series of profound themes including the ineffability of the source of life, the (feminine) creative aspect of the soul, achieving unity with the source of being, and the methods of discovering wisdom and maintaining humility.

The Thunder, Perfect Mind: A poem discovered among the Nag Hammadi manuscripts, recorded in Coptic but presumed to have been originally composed in Greek sometime in the second or third century. Availing itself of parallel strophes presenting paradoxical, riddling self-identifications, the text is written in the voice of the divine feminine (Sophia).

Trimorphic Protennoia: A Gnostic text from the New Testament Apocrypha, the Trimorphic Protennoia (The Three Forms of the First Thought) relates much the same cosmology as the Secret Book of John, though this time in the first-person voice of Barbelo, the agent of creation and the first "thought" of the Monad (that is, God in the sense of an ineffable and unknowable perfection).

Vinaya, Mahavagga: The Vinaya is a sacred Buddhist text, of which the Mahavagga forms a part; the Mahavagga contains accounts of the awakening of the Buddha and of his disciples along with guidelines for monastic behavior.

Wisdom of Solomon: One of the books of Deuteronomy included in the Septuagint. Though noncanonical in Rabbinic Judaism, the book has been canonized as part of the Christian Bible. Traditionally ascribed to Solomon, the text is thought to have been written in the Hellenistic period around 70 CE by an Alexandrian Jew. As a book of wisdom literature, the Wisdom of Solomon presents the character of Wisdom in personified form. The book is divided into six chapters and two parts. The first part deals largely with an address, or rebuke, to the rulers of the earth. The second contains an address by Wisdom to King Solomon, in which Solomon's life is recounted.

Bibliography and Suggestions for Further Reading

Blake, William. *The Complete Poems*. Edited by Alicia Ostriker. New York: Penguin Books, 1977.

Blofeld, John. *The Zen Teachings of Huang Po*. New York: Grove Press, 1958.

Burroughs, Kendra Crossen, annotator. *Bhagavad Gita: Annotated & Explained*. Translated by Shri Purohit Swami. Woodstock, VT: SkyLight Paths, 2001.

Ching, Tsai Chih. *Zen Speaks: Shouts of Nothingness*. Translated by Brian Bruya. New York: Anchor Books, 1994.

Davies, Stevan, trans. and annotator. *The Gospel of Thomas: Annotated & Explained*. Woodstock, VT: SkyLight Paths, 2013.

Earle, Mary C., annotator. *Celtic Christian Spirituality: Essential Writings—Annotated & Explained*. Woodstock, VT: SkyLight Paths, 2011.

———. *Julian of Norwich: Selections from* Revelations of Divine Love—*Annotated & Explained*. Woodstock, VT: SkyLight Paths, 2013.

Eknath, Easwaran. *God Makes the Rivers to Flow*. Tomales, CA: Nilgiri Press, 2003.

———. *Original Goodness*. Tomales, CA: Nilgiri Press, 1996.

Fox, Matthew. *One River, Many Wells: Wisdom Springing from Global Faiths*. New York: Tarcher/Penguin, 2004.

Gamard, Ibrahim, trans. and annotator. *Rumi and Islam: Selections from His Stories, Poems, and Discourses—Annotated & Explained*. Woodstock, VT: SkyLight Paths, 2004.

Hanh, Thich Nhat. *Being Peace*. Berkeley, CA: Parallax Press, 1987.

Helminski, Camille. *The Light of Dawn: Daily Readings from the Holy Qur'an*. Louisville, KY: Threshold Books, 1998.

Holman, John. *The Return of the Perennial Philosophy*. London: Watkins, 2008.

Huxley, Aldous. *The Perennial Philosophy: An Interpretation of the Great Mystics, East and West*. New York: Harper Perennial, 2009.

Kohn, Livia, trans. and annotator. *Chuang-tzu: The Tao of Perfect Happiness—Selections Annotated & Explained*. Woodstock, VT: SkyLight Paths, 2011.

Krishnamurti, Jiddu. *On God*. San Francisco: HarperSanFrancisco, 1992.

———. *Total Freedom: The Essential Krishnamurti*. New York: HarperCollins, 1996.

Kujawa-Holbrook, Sheryl, trans. and annotator. *Hildegard of Bingen: Essential Writings and Chants of a Christian Mystic—Annotated & Explained*. Woodstock, VT: SkyLight Paths, 2016.

Lin, Derek, trans. and annotator. *Tao Te Ching: Annotated & Explained*. Woodstock, VT: SkyLight Paths, 2007.

Maguire, Jack, annotator. *Dhammapada: Annotated & Explained*. Translated by Max Müller. Woodstock, VT: SkyLight Paths, 2005.

Miller, Ron, trans. and annotator. *The Sacred Writings of Paul: Selections Annotated & Explained*. Woodstock, VT: SkyLight Paths, 2007.

Moore, Thomas. *Gospel—The Book of Matthew: A New Translation with Commentary— Jesus Spirituality for Everyone*. Woodstock, VT: SkyLight Paths, 2016.

Mother Teresa. *In the Heart of the World*. Novato, CA: New World Library, 1997.

Paintner, Christine Valters, annotator. *Desert Fathers and Mothers: Early Christian Wisdom Sayings—Annotated & Explained*. Woodstock, VT: SkyLight Paths, 2012.

Roosevelt, Eleanor. *Universal Declaration of Human Rights*. Bedford, MA: Applewood Books, 2001.

Rosemont, Henry. *Is There a Universal Grammar of Religion?* Chicago: Open Court, 2008.

Schuon, Frithjof. *The Transcendent Unity of Religions*. Wheaton, IL: Quest Books, 2011.

Shapiro, Rami, trans. and annotator. *The Divine Feminine in Biblical Wisdom Literature: Selections Annotated & Explained*. Woodstock, VT: SkyLight Paths, 2013.

———. *Ecclesiastes: Annotated & Explained*. Woodstock, VT: SkyLight Paths, 2010.

———. *Ethics of the Sages:* Pirke Avot—*Annotated & Explained*. Woodstock, VT: SkyLight Paths, 2006.

———. *The Golden Rule and the Games People Play: The Ultimate Strategy for a Meaning-Filled Life*. Woodstock, VT: SkyLight Paths, 2015.

———. *Hasidic Tales: Annotated & Explained*. Woodstock, VT: SkyLight Paths, 2004.

———. *The Hebrew Prophets: Selections Annotated & Explained*. Woodstock, VT: SkyLight Paths, 2004.

———. *Proverbs: Annotated & Explained*. Woodstock, VT: SkyLight Paths, 2011.

Smith, Allyne. *Philokalia: The Eastern Christian Spiritual Texts—Selections Annotated & Explained*. Translated by G. E. H. Palmer, Philip Sherrard, and Kallistos Ware. Woodstock, VT: SkyLight Paths, 2008.

Smith, Andrew Philip, trans. and annotator. *The Lost Sayings of Jesus: Teachings from Ancient Christian, Jewish, Gnostic and Islamic Sources—Annotated & Explained*. Woodstock, VT: SkyLight Paths, 2006.

Smith, Huston. *Forgotten Truth: The Common Vision of the World's Religions*. San Francisco: HarperSanFrancisco, 1976.

Sultan, Sohaib N., annotator. *The Qur'an and Sayings of Prophet Muhammad: Selections Annotated & Explained.* Translated by Yusuf Ali. Woodstock, VT: SkyLight Paths, 2007.

Taylor, Rodney L., annotator. *Confucius, the Analects: The Path of the Sage—Selections Annotated & Explained.* Translated by James Legge. Woodstock, VT: SkyLight Paths, 2011.